THE QUINN IN ME

Volume 2

Quinn Kids on the Move

An Autobiography

ROSEMARY QUINN GABRIEL

Edited by JEANINE HANSEN

Front cover photo: Quinn Kids in Crane, IN 1943
Back cover photo by Shannon McMahan Designer Portraits:
http://shannonmcmahan.com

For Dad

You were like

a kite flying in all directions,

pulling us behind you on the tail...

all of us fluttering happily along.

Being with you was pure joy.

Rose Mary Queni Galil

10 - 4 - 21

Prologue

We were on the platform in the Chicago depot desperately trying to find our train to Pittsburgh. No one would stop to help and I can't imagine what was going through Mom's mind. She was holding ten-month-old Ann and I was hopping on one foot because I had sprained my ankle. I would be turning ten shortly after arriving in our new home. The rest of the kids started to scatter about. Pat was eleven, Joan, eight, John, five and Romaine was all of three. It was late October 1942.

Then Mom saw a porter hurrying toward us pushing a cart filled to the top with suitcases. "Pat, stop that porter! He'll know where we need to go."

"Kid, get outta my way. I've got to get these bags to their train, now," the porter said impatiently.

"My mom needs to talk to you," Pat said frantically. "We need help to find our train."

The porter looked at Mom and could see she really needed help – a woman travelling on her own with six kids. He pointed out the correct track for us to follow and was on his way. We hurried – *as fast as I could hop.* As we got closer, the engineer blew his whistle and rang the bell. The conductor called, *All Aboard!* and we began to panic. We were too far away to ever make that train.

"Pat, run as fast as you can and tell the conductor we're coming. Don't let that train leave without us," Mom said emphatically. She then encouraged us, "Hurry, hurry kids, we can't miss that train!"

I watched Pat run to where the conductor was standing. They exchanged words, and then Pat ran past him and jumped on the train. The conductor was waiving frantically for the engineer to stop the train. Then the conductor disappeared onto the train while we were still too far away to board. After a few more of my hops, he reappeared and motioned for us to hurry. He hadn't been able to catch Pat. He wasn't happy that we were so slow but could see we were really trying. By some miracle we all made it on the train before it left the station.

Relieved that we were all settled on the train, Mom was ready to answer Joan's questions, "Why are we going to this new place? Why is Dad there?"

Mom said, "Uncle Albert called to ask Dad to move to Pennsylvania. His company needed a bulldozer operator right away. That's why Dad left a month ago. They have the contract to remove the top off the mountain where the new Pittsburgh airport is going to be built." Uncle Albert was Dad's twin brother. I always thought it was funny that my dad's name was Alfred and his twin was named Albert. They became known as Big Al and Little Al to keep them apart.

Mom continued, "Your dad and I considered our situation in Markville. We had a good life and the store was doing well, but Markville is shrinking. People are moving away for better opportunities in bigger cities. We didn't know how long our little store could support our whole family. So we decided it was time to move and take advantage of this new opportunity. We found a buyer for the store and Dad was able to pack up and go to Pennsylvania. He needed time to look for a place for us to live.

"Dad has been staying at a farmhouse that is going to be torn down soon, but he is going to live with us again starting tonight. Isn't that great?"

Then Mom said, "Thank you, God." I thanked God, too. This train ride couldn't be over soon enough for me.

Finally, we were pulling into Pittsburgh Station. Now it was a rush to make sure we didn't leave any of our belongings behind. Mom warned us if we forgot something we'd never see it again, so we better check twice. Since we left most of our belongings behind, I tried to double check for everybody. Every item was now precious. Mom made sure we stayed in our seats until the rest of the passengers had gone down the aisle.

Waiting was awful. I was so tired of being on a train. I couldn't lie down, and most of the time I couldn't even put my foot up to ease my sprained ankle. My ankle was really swollen and my shoe hurt my foot. I thought to myself, *I'll never be so dumb to jump for a rope in a hay mow again.*

When we finally got to the door of the train, I saw Dad standing on the platform waiting for us. My heart leaped for joy! Now I knew everything would be okay. The conductor held my arm while the rest of the kids rushed to go hug Dad. The conductor helped me off the train and then turned to help Mom and Ann. I'm sure Mom never intended to ride a train again. I knew

I never did.

"Well, lady, we got you all here," the conductor said to Mom. "Sure looks like your man is happy to see this crew. You have lots of kids, but they weren't too much trouble." He laughed and handed Ann to Dad.

I was so happy I just hung on to Dad until it was time to go to the car. It was like being at home again just to be with Dad. Pat was always telling me not to be a cry baby, but guess what, he had tears in his eyes too. That whole month without Dad was unbearable.

We all scrambled to the old '36 Plymouth for the ride to our house. We were finally on our way to Moon Run. Anywhere would be a beautiful place to live, as long as Dad was there. I couldn't wait for morning to see this new town.

MOON RUN, PENNSYLVANIA
October 1942

1. Moon Run

It was a short trip from the train station to our new home and since it was dark I saw next to nothing of the countryside. The inside of our house was drab and had only one window in each room. This was far different from our home in Markville. The kitchen, dining room and living room were all one combined room. Dad had furnished it with a table and chairs. For kitchen cupboards, he had nailed together wooden dynamite boxes he had brought home from work. There was no running water in the kitchen. Dad told us there was a water pump up the hill from the front door. We would be sharing it with two other families for all of our water needs. No water meant no bathroom in the house either.

The next room was long and was furnished with two double beds, a twin bed and a crib for Ann. The double bed closest to the door was for Joan and me. The other double bed was for John and Romaine. Pat got the twin bed at the far end. There were no closets, only more dynamite boxes nailed together like in the kitchen. All of us kids would now be sharing one bedroom.

The third room was much smaller and would be Mom and Dad's bedroom. Same thing. There was a double bed and more dynamite boxes nailed together to serve as dressers. One chair by the bed completed the furnishings. I was in a state of shock, but I kept it to myself. Mom never complained either, even though things were primitive compared to back home in Minnesota. I guess she was just plain happy to be back together with Dad. All of us kids were glad to have Dad back in charge, too.

Dad took us back to our new bedroom, which had a door leading outside. He opened the door and pointed, "Look here, kids. That building is the outhouse. It has four doors. Ours is the one with the moon sawed out at the top. The others are for the rest of our neighbors living here."

I thought, *Oh, no! Joan is afraid of the dark. I guess I know who will go to the outhouse with her every time.* Dad stood by the door sending us out to use the outhouse before we went to bed. I was too tired to complain about going with Joan. She hurried, and so did I. We were all so exhausted from our trip that it didn't take long before we were all sleeping soundly, happy to be in comfortable beds.

When we got up in the morning there were more surprises and thankfully my ankle was feeling better. It was smoky and smelly outside. I looked out the door and saw an unbelievable landscape – it was almost as if I had been transported to another world. Our house was halfway up a hill, facing a valley filled with huge hills of black coal. Further down the hill on our side was what looked like a grass covered road. I learned it had been a railroad track to haul coal from the mines to market. The three local coal mines were closed long ago and that was why the tracks had been taken up and grass had taken over. What I thought were hills of coal were in reality what they called slag heaps.

The slag heaps were smoking and the smoke hung low in the sky causing a foul smell. It was a depressing sight. The only time we saw smoke back in Markville was when a steam engine train went through town. The smoke would disappear as soon as the train pulled out of town. Of course, there was smoke in the winter from all the stoves and furnaces, but they all burned wood so the smoke smelled good.

We ate breakfast and went exploring the area. From the outside of our home, I could tell that we were now living in a type of apartment – there were three in our building. This was coal miner housing. The coal mines had built housing for the workers and it was bare bones construction. They never even bothered to paint the outside so it looked like we were living in a barn with bare wood on the outside. The kids next door, Sonny and Dolly, laughed at our accent and we laughed at theirs. We would learn a whole bunch of new slang words for everyday words we were used to. This was going to be an adventure for us. We would be riding a school bus, have more than one teacher, and the school would furnish our pencils and paper tablets. Think of that! *Getting school supplies furnished by the school.* We couldn't wait to tell Mom of our good luck. We would start school the next day and I couldn't wait to see this wonderful place with all the changes.

The school was a square building with two floors. The lower grades occupied the lower floor and fourth, fifth and sixth grades were on the top floor. We changed rooms for different subjects, which made us feel completely grown up. The other students found it fun to try to copy our accent. We learned new words like *poke*, which is a paper bag; *soda*, any kind of pop; and if it was one mile or ten miles down the road they said it was *a piece away.*

2. The Slag Heaps

Every time Dad saw smoke rising from those ugly slag heaps, he warned us to stay off of them. He told us there was coal burning under the top crust, a crust that could be very thin or a couple of feet thick; no one could tell by looking at them.

We talked to the other kids and found out they ran around on top of the slag heaps all the time. None of them ever got in trouble, they said. There was no history of accidents or anyone getting hurt, they said. I figured that, more than likely, any kids involved in accidents on the slag heaps wouldn't tell, so nothing was reported.

I heard one of the high school boys, named Happy, daring two sixth grade boys to go for a top run on the slag heaps. They didn't seem interested until he called them scaredy-cat girls. They got braver the more he taunted. They agreed to meet right where they were standing on Saturday morning and "see what happens."

Pat and I wanted to be there to see who would back

down. Saturday came and we headed for the meeting place. As we walked toward the spot we could see four or five kids standing around talking.

"Look, there's a lot of smoke today. When it rained yesterday the coal started burning again," Pat said.

Sonny agreed with Pat.

"I hope they don't do it. It looks dangerous," I said.

Sonny said, "Fred isn't that brave. Besides, I think all four of them should go together. We should dare them to all go together."

We reached where they were standing in time to hear their plan. They had decided to run together so no one would be called chicken.

Happy was the spokesperson, as usual. He said, "We'll run from that high spot down to where Stu will be standing. It isn't who gets there first, it's who doesn't quit."

The four climbed up toward the starting spot. Most of us stayed where we were but Pat and Sonny followed the daredevils up to the top. A lot of talking was going on, but the runners hadn't started yet. Some of the kids on the old railroad track bed were yelling for them to get the race started. I was biting my lip, hoping it would keep the runners safe.

Then a bunch of kids started chanting, "Go-go-go-go---let's go-go-o-o!"

Off they went – running through the smoke. Suddenly the front runner, Happy, disappeared. The other runners stopped dead in their tracks. Then another runner disappeared, but I couldn't see who it was.

Now Pat started yelling, "Bring some boards!"

We were right next to an old building that was falling down and there were some loose boards lying around it. I grabbed a couple of boards and ran up the slag heap along with some other kids who were also scrambling to get boards to the top. I tried to hurry but kept losing my footing. It was as if gravity was working against me. When I finally got to the top I handed the boards to Pat and Sonny.

They laid on their stomachs and held the boards out as far as they could, reaching out to the two boys who had fallen into the smoking hole. I looked down and saw red coals. Ashes and coal had fallen around both of them. It was terrible. The boys were scrambling trying to reach the boards. I couldn't bear to look. A bigger boy came and slid down toward the terrified boys. Someone handed him a board to reach down to them.

Somehow, some way, those boys were rescued. Both had horrible burns all over their bodies. They looked terrified as they headed down the side of the heap toward safety. I was amazed at Pat's courage and quick thinking; he never hesitated to help and I was sure happy I was there to hand him boards. If we weren't there, those boys might have died.

I decided then and there that if I ever saw anyone climbing on the slag heaps again, I would yell at them to get down and tell them how dangerous it was. The sight of those two boys in the midst of burning coals haunted me for a long time.

Slag Heaps on the hill in Moon Run, PA in 2014.
Imagine what they looked like in 1942! Our house was just
behind the garage in the bottom right.
Photo Courtesy Chris Dellamea, coalcampusa.com

3. New Neighbors

We had lots of company over for meals and evening visits after supper back in Markville. We missed having friends over when we first moved to Moon Run. Before long, new family friends came by and we all sat around either on the porch or in the kitchen. Our new neighbors next door were the Mahoney's. Sonny was Joan's age and Dolly was a year older than me. Their mother, Mary, was about Mom's age and they had lots in common. Their father's name was Frank. The Clarks from two doors down were also visiting.

When the conversation slowed down, Frank Mahoney asked Dad, "You operate a bulldozer out at the new airport, don't you? Is that what you did back in Minnesota?"

"I did when I was real young and worked at a lumber camp in Wisconsin," Dad said. "But I was a postmaster before we came to Pennsylvania. Had a grocery store, too."

"That's a change. What do you like best?" Frank asked.

"Living in a real small town where everyone is your close neighbor and they help you keep track of your kids was a great life. But I have to admit, I love what I'm doing now, too. The bulldozers are bigger and more powerful than I've ever driven and we sure get the job done faster than ever before."

"You came a long way from Minnesota for this job. How does it pay?"

Dad replied, "It pays pretty good. Sure is a different life though. Being in the store I saw friends all day long. Now sometimes I only get to talk to three or four people and then I might only know one or two of them. I get home from work and it's already supper time. Makes for a very short day of seeing my kids."

Frank thought for a moment and said, "I work long days, too. Miss out on the family fun most of the time."

Dad had a melancholy look on his face. "I used to be able to take a kid or two with me if I had someplace to go."

"I don't even have a car," Frank replied. "When we go somewhere, it's not far from home."

I was standing there listening and realized that most of my new friends had never been further from home than Pittsburgh, only ten miles away. When we lived in Markville, we got to visit Grandpa and Grandma Quinn. They lived over one hundred miles away. Wow, even when I went to Beldon to visit Mrs. Hogan it was fifteen miles down the tracks. I guess I was lucky and had never realized it before.

I walked over to listen to what Mom and Mrs. Clark were saying. Mrs. Clark was holding her arm up to show Mom her new wrist watch. It was so pretty. I leaned in to see better. I admired it by saying, "Ooh" and "Ahh" a few times.

Mrs. Clark turned to me and said, "I don't have a

girl to give my old watch to. I'd like to give it to you if it's alright with your mom."

"That is so nice of you," Mom said to Mrs. Clark. Then she looked at me. "What do you say, Rose Mary? Would you like a watch?"

I smiled in disbelief. "Would I ever!"

Mrs. Clark dug around in her purse and came up with a ladies' watch that I fell in love with immediately.

"Here it is," she said. "It's been a good watch. Keeps great time. Now you can be the one everyone talks to. They'll all be asking you for the time. I always love saying, *It's exactly three-oh-two.*" She gave me a smile and a wink like we were now part of the same club.

"Thank you! Thank you!" I said as I gave her a big hug. "My own watch forever! I can't believe it!" I rushed over to show the kids my wonderful watch. I didn't sleep much that night because I had to make sure I really had my own watch.

I took care of that watch like it was my baby. I was very careful to make sure it never got wet. I took it off any time I was going to get my hands wet. The next night was bath night. I took my watch off and gently laid it next to my clothes on my bed. I took my bath and hurriedly dried off and got dressed. I turned around to put my watch on and it was gone! I panicked. *I was so careful to place it next to my clothing on the bed. Where could it have gone?*

I had tears in my eyes as I ran from Pat to Joan to Romaine to see if anyone had seen my watch. They hadn't seen it anywhere. Then I saw John sitting on the end of the porch. He was concentrating really hard on something he was holding in his hand. Then I saw it.

"My watch! What are you doing with my watch?" I cried. John had removed the back and was trying to do something on the inside. I was horrified. He certainly didn't know how to fix a watch at the age of eight.

I ran over to Dad and pleaded, "John is taking my new watch apart. He's going to wreck it! *Please* make him give it back, Dad!"

"I'll talk to him," Dad said as he walked toward John. "John Quinn, what do you think you're doing? Did you ask if you could touch Rose Mary's watch?"

John looked as innocent as an angel as he said, "I just wanted to see what makes the hands move. I'm not going to break it."

"You scared me to death!" I said. "I thought it was lost forever. You never ask – you just take things." I was crying in relief by now. At ten, this was a very serious issue to me.

John put my watch back together and handed it to me. Sure enough, it was still ticking. Dad made John apologize and promise not to touch it again without my permission. I was so relieved that it was still working that I forgave John instantly.

John was like that. If he was interested in something he would just take it apart to see how it worked. I guess that's why he could fix anything his whole life. He figured out how to make things work and could even make missing parts by hand. We never knew what John would take apart next, but he always figured out how to fix whatever he took apart, even at a young age.

4. The Mahoney's

It was really nice having the Mahoney's next door. I know Mom appreciated her friendship with Mrs. Mahoney, whose name was Mary. Mom didn't drive and the Mahoney's didn't own a car, which meant they both had to take the bus if they wanted to go somewhere during the day when Dad was at work. Mary taught Mom all the things she needed to know about the bus routes and how to get where she needed to go. If we wanted to go to Pittsburgh, we had to change buses in McKees Rocks, and so on.

Mr. Mahoney was a mystery to me. He worked at one of the steel mills in Pittsburgh. In the 1940's that was a terrible place to work. The heat was the worst of it. They worked in short shifts, allowing the workers to get away from the terrible heat for a few minutes, several times per shift. We never got to see Mr. Mahoney except on his days off. When he was home on his days off he mostly slept or tried to stay out of the heat.

Then one day he came home in the middle of the day. He stared straight ahead and couldn't manage to walk in a straight line, stumbling as he went. That was the first time in my life I had ever seen, or known, anyone that was drunk. He was a tall, slender man with reddish-brown fly away hair. He was always pushing that hair away from his forehead and it looked like he never combed it. He seemed to look right through us without saying a word. It scared us kids, and we made sure to stay out of his way.

I guess the heat and smell of the steel mill was enough to make even the best man need to forget it. I don't know how other mill workers handled it, but Mr. Mahoney chose a sad way, the bottle. I couldn't decide which was worse, the steel mill in Pittsburgh or the coal mine further down the valley. When I would see the miners walking home, black from the coal dust, carbide lamps on their hats, I couldn't imagine how they could keep going back to the mine day after day. It must have been so dusty, *so dark* down there. I hope their families understood what a hard job it was.

Dolly and Sonny both ran to their grandma's house to stay for a "few days" when their dad was on a binge. She lived in a house across the empty field we played in. It was a known fact that when Mr. Mahoney went on a binge, he got mean. He enjoyed fighting and wasn't above giving Mary a slap or two, just because. Dad told us, "When Mr. Mahoney isn't himself, everyone play on the other side of the house. I don't want you around him when he's on his way home from the bar."

That included Dolly and Sonny. Mr. Mahoney was a hardworking man who drank to make his life livable but forgot how the binges destroyed his family. They were afraid of him, too. When Dolly and Sonny came back from their grandma's house I asked them why they had stayed for two days.

Dolly said, "We always stay long enough for Dad to go back to work. He gets better and then we feel safe at home again."

Sonny told us, "When Dad is well he's sorry and tells us he won't get drunk again. That lasts for a month or two. Then we go to stay with Grandma for a while. Dad is never mean around Grandma."

When I saw Mary with bruises on her face, I didn't like it. It seemed like a bad dream and I was thankful it never happened at our house.

5. Junk Store Junkies

When we moved to Pennsylvania it was a whole new world. I had been to Minneapolis and Sioux Falls, but they were nothing like Pittsburgh. The traffic was terrible, all because of the three rivers. Everywhere we went, we had to try to find a bridge. I went in to Pittsburgh on the bus with Mom a few times, but the real fun was going with Dad.

Dad was a junk store junkie. We would spend the whole day going from junk store to junk store. Sometimes he was looking for a special item and sometimes he just wanted to spend the day looking to see what he could find. We needed things for the house because we had left everything but our clothes with our Aunt Rose and Uncle Ralph.

Dad would start up a conversation with the clerk, who was usually the owner, and I'd get to roam around checking out all the neat stuff...things I had never seen before; things so mysterious I'd either take them to Dad for an answer or I'd drag him back deep in the shop to tell me what they were. I learned about parts of cars, building supplies, gardening tools, hospital equipment, old uniforms, guns, barbed wire, horse shoes, saddles, bridles, and on and on.

One time we were looking for a washing machine. With six kids, Mom needed a washer that did a good job. We started in McKees Rocks, the next town over to the east from Moon Run. We found a washer in almost every store we stopped at. We started making rounds for a second time, with Dad telling each owner that we had found a washer at a better price at some other shop.

He'd say, "I wish you could sell me your washer at the same lower price because I really like this washer better than the other one."

This went on at several stores and I was getting tired of going back to the same stores all over again. That's when Dad told me his secret: "You have to be a horse trader. You have to decide which washer you like best and then run around getting better prices so when you go back to the shop where your choice is, you'll have a better price to throw at them. Sometimes it works and then again, sometimes it doesn't. The owner usually knows what his washer is worth and how he has it priced compared to the others."

When we finally got back to the store where he wanted to buy the washer, he opened the door and we started to head in the shop.

We heard a voice yell from the back, "Don't even come in! We all talked about you running around getting us to bid against each other. None of us will sell you a washer today." I thought, *Oh no - we will have to go home without a washer today. What will Mom think?*

Dad just started to laugh and said, "Okay, tomorrow it is. I want to buy the washer you have so I'll be back tomorrow. Come give me your best price or my daughter will have to go without new shoes for another week."

The man came up to the front of the store laughing. "Okay, okay, you win. You have broken my heart with your daughter's poor feet. What price did I tell you last?"

Dad got the washer for a good price and we headed happily on our way. I was beaming.

I don't remember how much Dad paid for the washer, but I learned that you can break down even the hardest heart by never giving up. Dad made up his mind of what he was willing to pay and worked on the shop owners until he got his price. By the end of that shopping spree, I was ready to get out of the junk stores for a while and get on to something else.

6. Shopping in Pittsburgh

Mom and Mary Mahoney loved taking the bus in to Pittsburgh to shop at the big department stores. Dolly and I always begged to go along, but it rarely happened.

One Saturday we got to go. It was right before Easter and we both would be getting a new dress to wear to church on Easter Sunday. We thought we were the luckiest girls in the whole state. After walking up the hill beside our house to the bus stop we waited impatiently for the bus to come. Dolly and I got to sit in a seat by ourselves on the bus to McKees Rocks. We changed buses and sat with our moms on the way to Pittsburgh from there. All we could talk about was how we would look when we got our new dresses.

Downtown Pittsburgh is a maze of buildings, streets, and of course the three rivers. The Allegheny and Monongahela join to form the start of the Ohio River right there in the center of the city. It would be easy for us to get lost among the short streets, rivers and all of the different doors of the big stores. Dolly and I were so busy looking around that we kept lagging about half a block behind our moms. They told us more than once that it would be our last trip if we didn't do a better job of keeping up and staying close.

We did fine until we got into Macy's. That's when I saw some jewelry I just had to take a look at. I loved bracelets and was bending down to look closer. When I looked up, no one was in sight. I stood there looking around for a minute waiting to see a familiar face. I walked around the counter, and walked around it again. Still, no one. I hadn't paid attention to which door we entered the store so I couldn't decide which one to go out. I was ten and had never been lost before. I had never worried about finding my way home.

I guess I was too naive to be afraid. We kids were on our own all the time back home in Markville – we never even thought of being scared. It was always easy to find our way home in a small town.

In the meantime, Mom was starting to panic. Mary was telling her about how dangerous it was for kids in the city, especially girls. That surely wasn't what Mom wanted to hear while I was wandering around downtown Pittsburgh by myself.

While they were becoming more frantic, I calmly walked to the closest door and out onto the street. I thought, *Which way should I go? It doesn't matter, I will either catch them or run into them while I'm looking around.* I decided to look into each door as I came to them. Macy's had lots of doors and it was taking me extra time to go and look inside each one. Door one, no luck. Door two, no luck, and so on around the block. I finally got to the door where I started and then it occurred to me that I might be in trouble.

26

By being in trouble, I meant that Mom might not ever take me shopping again. I was the true description of a window shopper. I stopped to look in every window, every counter, in every store where we shopped. I must admit, I spent more time looking in windows than I did looking for Mom and the others.

Mom and Mary were getting desperate. They started asking people on the street if they had seen a girl wandering around looking lost. No luck. They had Dolly by the hand dragging her along as fast as she could go. She started crying and complained about the way they treated her when she hadn't done anything wrong.

I got tired of walking so I stopped to admire the toys in one of the windows when suddenly I felt someone grab my shoulder. I turned around to see fire in Mom's eyes and tears running down her cheeks. I had never seen her look so frightened. My heart sank and I felt sick to my stomach. It never entered my mind that she'd be worried for my safety. It was a real lesson for me to know that I had caused them all so much worry. Of course, I never really understood what I put Mom through until years later when I had kids of my own. I had been wandering around on my own for close to an hour.

I thought for sure we would be heading straight home because Mom was so mad, but being the tenderhearted person that she was, she still bought me an Easter dress. Dolly got hers, too. If it hadn't been for Dolly counting on a new dress I bet I would have missed out for sure. I don't remember Dolly's dress but mine was so beautiful. I never dreamed I'd get a store bought dress. This dress was white with pink flowers and had a large white collar with lace around it. The fabric was shiny like silk and felt slippery to the touch.

I grew up a lot that day. I learned to be concerned about other people's feelings in the future. Thankfully, I was safe and sound. Dolly and I both felt like princesses at church on Easter morning in our new dresses.

7. Fighting the Bullies

Pat and I continued to rely on each other as best friends, although more and more we had our own friends. One time we were walking on the road by the slag heaps when two bigger boys we didn't know stopped to talk to us. One was a redhead not much bigger than Pat. The other boy was huge. The more they talked the more belligerent they became. One of them gave Pat a little shove. Pat put up his fists and offered to fight him. Just then the other boy gave Pat a shove, too. Now both put up their fists to fight.

"That's not fair! One fight at a time," I told them.

"You stay out of this. You're just a girl," the red-head told me. "Girls don't know how to fight."

"I can too fight, can't I Pat?"

"You stay out of this. I can fight my own battles. These two don't scare me," Pat warned me.

"You're just a skinny little kid. You probably need help, especially from a girl," shot back the big guy.

"You swing first or get out of our way," Pat said coolly through clenched teeth.

The redhead stepped back but the fat guy took a swing and that's all it took. The fight was on. I was yelling and pushing the redhead while Pat and the big guy were swinging away. Pat was little, but he was quick. He got in two or three blows to every one the other kid landed. The redhead gave me a shove and I fell down on my hands and knees. That really got Pat fired up. He knocked the big guy down and took on the redhead. He landed a couple of more punches and the two bullies ran away.

Those two told all the other boys about how good Pat could fight. From then on Pat was the target for all the creeps and bullies who wanted to be the big man around town. It was a good thing Dad had given Pat all those boxing lessons back in Markville when he was training boys for prize fighting. Somehow Pat found friends to keep the fights fair and he kept on winning. Most of the time I was there trying to help, but Pat thought I was just in the way. He didn't need me, but I wanted him to win every time.

After a while the bullies left Pat alone, which made me happy. It seemed that no matter where we lived Pat had to fight to prove that he could. He was so much smaller than the other boys they must have thought he was an easy target. I managed to be there to cheer him on and complain if the fight wasn't fair. We always stuck together and we still do.

8. Miss McCain

Our whole elementary school back in Markville was two rooms, so it was a big change going to school in Moon Run. We had a whole classroom for each grade. We changed rooms for different subjects because the teachers only taught one subject. I thought that was strange – imagine a teacher only knowing enough to teach one thing.

Pat and I were both in the fifth grade and we felt completely lost. We were in different home rooms and hardly saw each other most of the day during school. Back in Markville, we sat next to each other all day and did our homework together.

We got used to this new way pretty quickly, and even started to like the system. I got along with all my teachers but one. She taught my favorite subject – history. I don't know why, but history was like living in a movie to me. When I read about times past it was easy to imagine being a part of that time and place. I guess that's why I remember the details of history so easily and clearly. My fifth grade history teacher, Miss

McCain, did not like me. I'm not sure why. Maybe she viewed me as a country hick because of how I dressed. I wore long, thick brown stockings to school every day. I had to wear a garter belt to keep them up above my knees. Since I was a sickly kid I had to stay warm at all times. My clothes were homemade, while all the other kids dressed like city kids with store-bought clothes.

Some of her favorite students would call her *Crabapple McCain* or *Old Maid McCain* behind her back because she was just plain mean-spirited. Miss McCain had a habit of passing out graded tests in her own cruel way. She would start with the lowest score and then work up to the highest score as she passed them out to each student, making remarks about the grades as she went. I usually was in the higher grades, but had never gotten the best score.

One day, Miss McCain started complaining that no one in the class had gotten 100% on the test except one student. Then she started her routine of disclosing the worst grade. Bobby had failed with a 64%.

"Alice, you were almost as bad," she said as she laid Alice's paper on her desk. She had gotten 69%.

I was sure that I had earned the only 100%. I could hardly wait until she finally praised me in front of the class. As she got to the students who usually had the best grades, she seemed to get more belligerent instead of happier because of their better grades. She told them she couldn't believe none of them had gotten 100%. Finally, she had one paper left in her hand.

Everyone knew it was mine.

She huffed, "Well, all of you whom I thought would get the 100% failed to do so. Someone you'd never expect to do that well, did. I can't believe you failed me." She stopped in front of my desk, held my paper up high, made a disgusted face and threw my test on the floor! I was so hurt I started to cry. One of the boys started to pick it up.

"Let it lay there," she said sharply. Then she turned around to her desk and sat down.

My hard-earned 100% paper lay there on the floor until class was over and all the students had left the room except me. She stood up, turned to the black-board and told me to leave. I picked up my paper and left in silence, absolutely crushed.

To this day, I can't forget what she did, or forgive her for the way she treated me. I wish I could have gone to the principal to complain so that no other students would have to be mistreated like that. Any teacher who treated students that way should be denounced for their prejudices.

9. Long, Tall Scoop of Ice Cream

When we lived in Markville, Ferdie came to town every Sunday to show the latest movie he had. The town hall became our movie theater, with chairs set up so everyone in town could watch. After the movie was over, everyone would stay for a lunch. It was the only entertainment in town, outside of church events, so most people went to the movie every week.

Now that we were in Moon Run, we had to go about five miles away to McKees Rocks to see movies in a regular theater. Mom and Dad would give each of us a quarter to go to the Saturday matinee. The quarter bought us a bus ticket for five cents, a movie ticket for twelve cents and a bus ticket back to Moon Run, unless we thought the weather was nice enough to walk home.

There was an Isaly's Ice Cream shop right by the theater and it was awesome. The shop was long and narrow, with a long display case containing at least fifteen flavors ready to be scooped. The other side had tables ready for customers who wanted to relax and enjoy their ice cream cone, sundae or banana split. The long aisle was wide enough for us all to walk back and forth looking over all the flavors before we could decide what we wanted that day. I absolutely loved ice cream. I wished I could eat ice cream every day. It used to take me a long time to decide because I wanted to try every flavor.

Isaly's cones were amazing, too. They were called Skyscrapers. Instead of the round mound of ice cream we were used to getting, theirs were skinny and tall. They had special scoops that looked like long, narrow, pointed trawls. These scoops made the greatest ice cream cone you ever saw. It may not have been more ice cream, but the illusion was impressive. I made my cone last as long as possible. When everyone else was finished with theirs, I managed to have at least one bite remaining. All this for five cents.

With only three cents left, we had to walk home. Of course, we country kids were used to walking everywhere, so we had no problem giving up the ride home for such a treat. We would walk along the railroad bed, which was a shortcut compared to walking along the road. We could amble along eating our ice cream without causing any traffic jams. It was fun to walk home after seeing a cowboy movie and a chapter from a Saturday serial.

Sometimes Dad would take us in to Pittsburgh to drive past the steel mills so we could see fire in the smelting furnaces. I was most impressed by the huge smoke stacks and large buildings connected to the steel mills.

Before we knew it, school was out for the summer and we had time to do a lot of nothing. We usually turned nothing into something, like the time Pat wanted to get a job.

10. Pat Gets a Job

Pat was always looking for ways to make money. He was really interested when Dave, one of the older boys, was bragging about the money he was earning as a caddy at the golf course. He waved the bills in front of a group of boys, showing off. The boys were impressed, especially Pat.

That night at supper, Pat asked Dad if he could look into being a caddy. Dad wanted to think it over. Even though Pat would be making money, he would have to hitchhike five or six miles to the golf course. Pat had finished fifth grade, but he was small for a boy of twelve. Weighing in at eighty pounds was a disadvantage for a caddy.

Dad said he would go to the golf course and talk to the manager to see if there was a job Pat could do. Pat was really anxious to be a caddy, so this made him happy. The next day, Dad drove to the golf course and talked to the manager. They both agreed that Pat could give it a try. Pat was thrilled, but Mom wasn't happy. She was sure that Pat was too small to carry a big bag of golf clubs around for nine holes, let alone eighteen, but Pat was determined.

Pat found Dave and made arrangements to go try caddying the next time Dave was on the schedule. Pat tagged along several times, looking forward to getting out on the course. Every time he went, all the other boys got picked to caddy except Pat. But Pat was determined that he could be a great caddy. Anyone else would have given up, but Pat kept going to the course with hopes that he would finally be picked. Pat and Dave would get to the course early, Dave and all the others would get picked. Pat would stay and wait until Dave was done, and then they would hitchhike home.

In the early forties there were no golf carts or pull carts. Golfers either had to hire a caddy or carry their clubs themselves. Golfers needed a caddy and Pat knew it.

We all thought Pat would quit before he even got started as a caddy. Then one day while he was waiting for Dave, two older men – Pat said they were *really old* – showed up to play. They needed a caddy – really two caddies between the two of them. Pat got excited because there were no other caddies around to steal his chance this time. The two men looked at Pat, then discussed the situation between themselves as they eyed the scrawny looking, eager-eyed Pat.

One of the men chuckled and said, "You look willing enough. Are you ready to give this a try?"

Pat quickly replied with a wide grin, "You bet!" He didn't want to give them a chance to change their minds.

"We really want to play, so we'll take turns carrying the bags. Maybe between the three of us we can make it around nine holes. I'm Bud and this is Steve."

"I'm Pat Quinn, soon to be the best caddy on the

course!"

"Nice to meet you, Pat. Let's get going."

Off they went, taking turns lugging the heavy bags of clubs and getting to know each other. Pat was about as stubborn an Irishman as they come, and he wasn't about to show any sign of struggle as he carried the heavy bags. He joked around and kept the two men entertained as they made it around the course.

When they finished the ninth hole, Bud and Steve shook Pat's hand.

Bud said, "Pat, you did a great job! I do believe you will be the best caddy on this golf course. From now on, you are our caddy. We will hire you any time we see you here. If there are two caddies available, we'll hire two, but you are our first choice."

It was true. They always hired Pat and so did other golfers as the word got around of how good and entertaining a caddy Pat was. Pat spent the rest of the summer making money, most of which he saved. I guess when you work that hard for money, it's too precious to spend.

11. Exploring

One summer day when Pat was not caddying, he and Sonny were looking for something to do. They had been across the valley searching the woods.

"You know what? Maybe the blackberries are ripe. We could pick some for a pie," Pat said.

"I'd rather take a gunny sack and bring home apples," said Sonny. "They may be ready, too."

"I want to go, too," I said. "You guys can use some help, can't you?" I had a squint in my eye, hoping they would say yes.

Sonny looked at Pat, nodded his head and said, "Sure, if you can keep up. You can always just come home whenever you want."

It was agreed that I could go along, which made me really happy. I admired my big brother and loved tagging along with him wherever he went. We ventured across the creek and on up the hill. The berries and apples were ready. But of course we didn't stop there, we still had adventuring to do. We climbed further on up the hill until we reached an old coal mine entrance. The opening was covered with a few rotting boards to keep adventurous kids like us out. One board said, DANGER. KEEP OUT. DO NOT ENTER.

It was easy to see that people had ignored the sign plenty of times and had entered to go exploring beyond the boards. We decided we wanted to see what was back there, too. Why should everyone else get all the fun?

Pat, Sonny and I crawled through the boards. Once inside we stood still for a couple of minutes, letting our eyes adjust to the darkness. It quickly became apparent it was time to form a plan since we could only go a few feet without a flashlight or torch.

Disappointed, but determined, we headed out to pick blackberries. There were more than enough berries to fill our buckets and our stomachs. We then picked a bunch of apples to fill our gunny sacks, and headed toward home.

We made a plan to return to the mine as soon as we could find a flashlight so we could explore further. It wasn't as easy as we thought. We owned one flashlight, which Dad kept in the car for emergencies, so that was out of the question. Sonny said they didn't have one and he even checked with his Aunt Millie and she didn't either. Our only hope was a torch. I had never seen a torch, but how hard could it be to make one?

We met the next day, planning how we could explore deeper into the mine. Sonny brought some matches. Pat had a stick, some paper, small nails and a tack hammer. Me, I had hope. The boys built the torch while I watched, anticipating our adventure.

We headed across the valley, back up the hill and

crawled inside the mine entrance. Sonny lit a match. It went out. He lit another. It went out, too.

"We better get back from this entry a ways. There's too much wind here," Pat said.

"Grab the stuff. We'll go back as far as we can go and still see. That should get us away from the wind," Sonny chimed in.

We headed deeper into the mine until we could hardly see each other anymore and Sonny lit another match.

"There's only two matches left. Are we ready to light the torch?" he said. The match he was holding went out.

"Okay, it's now or never," Pat said as he held up the makeshift torch where he had nailed the paper to the stick and Sonny lit another match. The torch quickly caught fire and we had bright light. We took a few quick steps further into the mine and suddenly our light was gone. We didn't realize how quickly the paper would burn out – I wish we had thought about that before. We had gotten far enough back in the mine that we could no longer see any light from the entrance in the distance. I was scared! I could hear Pat and Sonny breathing. They were listening. We stood there hoping that when our eyes got used to the dark we would see something, anything. But it was too dark – there was no way our eyes were going to adjust.

Pat took a deep breath and said, "That was fun. I just wish that we had more paper. Let's start walking out of here. I can see a little – can you?"

I lied and said I could see. They didn't believe me but didn't question me. We slowly started feeling our way toward the entrance. I found the wall. I was behind Pat and Sonny when I heard a sound like a rock falling.

"What was that?" I whispered.

"You must have kicked a rock," Pat said quietly.

"No, I didn't. Besides, it was toward the entrance. What was it?"

I heard Sonny's frightened voice, "I heard it too. I don't like it. Maybe the whole place is going to cave in on us. I wish we could see where we're going."

"You two babies – stop thinking the worst! So what if a piece of coal falls from the ceiling. That doesn't mean the whole thing is going to fall." Pat was talking in his grown-up voice, but I was sure he was scared, too.

I heard what sounded like several pieces of coal falling. I was terrified and tried my hardest to hold back the tears that started burning my eyes. Sonny was as scared as I was and began running. We heard him fall down. Pat and I hurried to try and catch him. I ran into the wall and hurt my elbow on the sharp rock. Somehow we finally got to where we could see enough not to fall down any more.

I heard more coal falling, but now we were closer to the sound and it didn't sound right. We made it to the entrance and heard somebody laughing. We stopped in our tracks. Who was laughing?

Outside the mine entrance were two older boys I didn't know, rolling on the ground laughing, holding their sides.

"We sure got you babies! Scared babies! When Jake threw that rock into the mine, did you wet your pants? Did you cry like girls?" he mocked us.

"You guys think you're so smart. We couldn't see when our torch went out so we were being careful not to run into the wall on the way out," Pat bluffed.

The boys told us they saw us cut across the valley and thought we were going to pick blackberries. They were going to pretend to be a bear and scare us out of the berry patch. It turned out far better when we went into the mine. They couldn't wait to get back and tell everyone how much they scared us.

The other kids laughed at us, but as always happened, someone else was worth picking on after a few days and we went on looking for our next adventure.

12. Moving to Crane, Indiana

When we moved to Moon Run, I thought we would live there for a long time. After all, I had only lived in one other place my entire life. Was I ever in for a surprise. We all knew Uncle Albert and his family lived in a house trailer so they could move from state to state as Uncle Albert continued to work for The Meyers Company.

Moon Run was really starting to feel like home. We had made good friends and were having fun getting used to the way things were done. Then one day, Dad came home and told us kids, "I'll be going to start a new job in about a week."

I asked, "A new job? Where? Will we be moving?"

Dad answered, "My new job is in Indiana in a town call Crane. Yes, we're moving."

I guess if we wanted to have Dad with us, moving was our new way of life. I couldn't imagine anything worse than living without Dad again for any amount of time, so I wasn't going to argue about it.

Mom didn't say anything. I bet they had talked about the move before Dad told us kids. We were day to day kids living in a new style of life. As long as it was okay with Mom and Dad, we didn't worry too much about what was next for us.

Here it was, less than a year after we arrived in Moon Run and we were packing to move to Indiana. It was an exciting move. The first thing I learned was that Dad would be working for the Navy. There's no place for the Navy to sail a ship in Indiana. That's what everyone said when we told them we were moving to Indiana. Dad had some explaining to do.

I asked Dad lots of questions; "Why did the Navy hire you, Dad? What are you going to do? Aren't you too old to join the Navy?" I wanted answers. Two of Dad's brothers were in the Army, serving in the Pacific. I didn't want Dad to have to go over there.

Dad said, "The Navy has an ammunition storage facility in Indiana and it needs to be enlarged. The Navy hired The Meyers Company to do the work. All of us are moving to Crane. The Navy built the town especially for the people who work at the storage facility. I am too old to join the Navy. Besides, I have too many kids! I'm just right to operate a bulldozer that will dig out the ground for the foundation in the underground munitions area."

That explained a lot. I did think of a lot more questions, but Dad couldn't answer them because the answers were *a not for publication secret*. I did find out that we would be living in a new house, in a new town, with new schools, stores and a community center. Everyone there would be new, just like us. I didn't realize what a big project this was for the Navy. It was 1943 and World War II was raging on. The big shells and torpedoes needed a safe place to be stored. The perfect spot was in the middle of our country almost a thousand miles from the Atlantic and more than two thousand miles from the Pacific.

Just like when we left Markville, Dad would go to his job first and Mom had to do all of the packing. It was hard to tell all of our friends that we were moving already. It was easy for me to make new friends, but some of my brothers and my sister Joan weren't very good at it.

Joan didn't want to move. She was sure she wouldn't like it there. That's what I heard every night when we went to bed. Back in Markville, when Joan wasn't even two years old, she was dropped on her head on the sidewalk and her eyes crossed so badly that she had to wear very strong eyeglasses with glass as thick as Coke bottles.

Someone told Dad about a specialist in Pittsburgh that could help Joan's eyes. Mom and Dad were always ready to do whatever it took to take care of us and improve our health. An appointment was made right away, and Joan went to see the specialist.

They came home with good news. The doctor ordered that a cover would be put over Joan's bad eye. It was a hard case that fit inside her glasses. It had a very small hole in the center for some light to enter allowing that eye to get some use. The doctor explained that it wouldn't be a quick fix.

The kids now had something new to tease Joan about – her eye patch that looked nothing like a Pirate's patch. I don't remember how long it took, but after a while that patch was switched out for a smaller one. Gradually her eye improved enough so that the patch could be removed altogether. By then she was in the fourth grade.

"I don't want to move. I won't like Indiana. The kids will laugh at me and my glasses and my awful patch," Joan complained over and over.

She was wearing her patch over her bad eye and her other eye wasn't much better. It was so bad she had to put her face almost on the book when she tried to read. The kids all teased her. I felt bad for her and tried not to think about Joan having to go through a move again. She tried very hard not to let it bother her, but she was still embarrassed by the mean things people said about her.

We were all packed and moving day came at last. When Dad arrived with the big moving truck, loading was easier than it had been in Markville. The biggest improvement was the boxes. Those dynamite boxes that we had used for cupboards made great moving boxes and Dad got as many as we needed from the jobsite. They stacked the boxes and the rest of our belongings in the back of the truck, which was a flat bed with wooden slatted sides. Dad managed to make a space by the tailgate for all of us kids to ride there. All except Ann; she was riding in front with Mom and Dad.

Dad fixed it up so we could play cards or read and study. He put a pile of blankets and pillows arranged so we could take a nap whenever we felt like it. We also had a box filled with sandwiches, fruit and crackers. That way we would only need to take bathroom breaks.

Before we hit the road, Dad called a meeting. He had a serious face as he told us the rules for our behavior. He looked at each one of us.

"Pat, RoseMary, Joan, Romaine and John, listen up – here are your rules for the trip: first, no fighting. Second, don't eat everything before we get out of Pennsylvania. The most important rule of all – don't try to look out of the truck after I get this canvas tied down. We are not supposed to let you ride in the back of this truck on the highway."

We all nodded our heads in agreement and promised to behave. Dad tied the canvas down over top of us and down the road we went. We kept our promise until we got on the highway. First, John, age six, could look out where the canvas was folded and there was a small gap. Then Pat decided to try to make the gap bigger so he could see, too. We stopped for a bathroom break and when Dad tied the canvas back down he didn't get it perfect like the first time. We all took turns looking out. We got brave and started waving at cars coming up behind us. They would smile and wave back. We were having a lot of fun and it made the time fly by.

We made a game of it. Pat was making faces. I thought I was so smart, I showed one car a sandwich, another an apple. They all seemed to like the things we did. We didn't know it, but some of the people in the cars were waving at Dad. When they motioned to him he got suspicious.

He stopped and came back to talk to us. As soon as he saw the canvas he knew what we were up to. He gave us a new lecture and we understood we were in serious trouble.

"Knock it off!" came through loud and clear. We got it. In those days a spanking was the norm and we did not want Dad to spank us. That was it – our fun was shut down. We were back to being bored for the rest of the ride. Fortunately, we were almost there by the time Dad was on to us. We traveled about four hundred and forty miles in the back of a big moving truck that day. Can you imagine that happening today?

CRANE, INDIANA
August 1943

13. Fun in Crane

When we finally arrived, we couldn't wait to see our new house. Dad untied the canvas and we all piled out and ran inside. I couldn't believe my eyes! All of us kids were running around like crazy, cheering at our good fortune.

It was a brand new house with a gas stove, a refrigerator, gas heat, hot and cold running water and even a bathroom complete with a bathtub! No more loading coal into the stove to cook or heat water for our baths in the washtub! No more hauling water in from the pump! Thank you, Lord, no more running to the outhouse on cold winter nights! There was a telephone, too. I felt like I had died and gone to heaven. I wanted to pinch myself to be sure I wasn't dreaming.

The next day, Dad took us exploring around town. Our house was on a circle drive along with three other homes. There were circle drives all around us with white houses lined up everywhere. All of the houses in town were white and gleamed in the sun they were so shiny and new. At the center of town was a square with the school, recreation center, post office, a couple of stores and a church. The Catholic Church was on base, so Dad told us we had to get Navy clearance to go to church on Sundays.

Yes, this new adventure in Crane, Indiana was going to turn out just fine.

Just like Dad said, the Navy built houses and businesses for the residents of Crane. The most popular hangout for us kids was the recreation center. My favorite thing there was the juke box, and it was free! We could push any numbers and a song would play. *In the Mood* by Glen Miller was my favorite. Joan and I made up our own Jitterbug routine. We wore out the record we practiced so much. Everyone else at the center was more than happy about that – they were sick of it by then.

There were lots of other things to do, too. Bingo was popular. The gym was busy at all hours with basketball, volleyball and running. There was a multipurpose room, called the Big Room, where we had lunches, parties and movie night once a week. We could also meet our friends to do homework, but there was usually more laughing going on than work getting done in the Big Room.

Church services were also held in the Big Room. The Navy Chaplain was Catholic and he preferred to hold services on base, so he held only one Mass, which is why we had to go on base for church. We felt special because we didn't know any other kids who went on base for church. One time I sat next to a Captain. I wanted to ask him what ship he Captained, but I knew Dad would frown if he saw me bothering the Captain so I kept my question to myself. One of my goals in life was to behave in a manner so Dad would never frown at me.

The base was a restricted area. All who entered needed a badge. Of course, Dad had a badge because he worked on base. He was one of the workers building the bunkers to protect the surrounding area in case any of the ammunition stored there would explode. I thought it was strange that the Navy had its torpedoes and bomb shells stored in the middle of Indiana.

We were all enjoying the rest of our summer, getting to know our new friends and neighbors. Since everyone who lived in Crane was a new resident, no one felt out of place or poorer than anyone else.

14. Joan to the Rescue

It's a good thing the summers weren't longer. John took Romaine everywhere and constantly got them both in fights. They liked to explore beyond their fixed boundaries and had no problem spouting their opposing opinions to one and all. This caused regular opportunities for a fight. Sometimes the fights were fair and sometimes they weren't. That's when John called in the big gun.

One day, John and Romaine were out walking around when they ran into a group of kids who seemed to be looking for a fight.

"You're just some dummy from Minnesota. Are all kids from Minnesota as dumb as you?" asked one of the bullies.

"You just wait. You can't call us names!" John yelled back at him.

"I can, too - any name I like. How about dumb hick? Do you like that better?" the bully taunted back.

"You better leave us alone. I'll go get my sister," John said, not backing down.

"Your sister? That's a laugh! Go get her – we'll wait," the bully replied.

John kept his eye on the bully and said, "Romaine, go get Joan. She'll settle these guy's bacon. Just don't do anything until Joan gets here. She makes people pay when they pick on me."

Romaine ran off to get Joan.

"Joan, Joan, we need help! Hurry up! They're going to beat John up," Romaine said when he found Joan.

Joan was clearly irritated. "Why does John always have to fight? I'm playing now. I'll come in a while."

Romaine wouldn't give up. "These guys came along and called us hicks from Minnesota. What's a hick?"

"Oh, all right. No one can call us names. I don't know what a hick is but they can't call us that. I'll make them take it back."

Joan and Romaine ran back to where John was, still arguing with the bullies. When the bullies saw Joan coming, they laughed.

"This is your sister? What a joke. She couldn't hurt a fly. Look at her. She's a four-eyed hick!" the bully taunted. They were all laughing until Joan started swinging.

She flew into them with both arms in motion. Her fists landed on any body part that got in the way. Her jaw was set and teeth clenched tight, daring anyone to swing back. The boys were so surprised they started backing up. Three boys against one girl with a purpose and they didn't have a chance. It only took one attack and they were running backwards.

"You can't call us names! You quit picking on my brothers and we are not HICKS, whatever a hick is," Joan shouted as she kept swinging her arms in windmill fashion. Watching Joan fight was like watching a great force in motion. You did not want to get in her way.

Joan turned to talk to John and Romaine.

"Can't you two keep out of trouble?" she asked. "I don't like to beat up boys all the time."

Romaine answered, "We didn't start it. They said, *Where do you dummies live? and Who said you could walk down our street?* That's when John called them goof balls."

Joan was angry. "I wish you two would do your own fighting. If I get one more rip in a dress Mom says I'll have to stay in the house."

John retorted, "We never start the fights. People just pick on us. We can't help it if they like to fight," and so on and so on all the way back to the house. John kept telling Joan all the reasons for fighting. Then she gave them both *the look*.

"How about ignoring the bullies? Next time I'm not coming."

That was the way it went every time trouble came along. I think Joan liked to fight. Every time they called for help, Joan would run to the rescue. They went through this every time we moved. It must have been a kid thing. Myself, I didn't want to fight. I kept my mouth shut. Well, most of the time.

15. On the Move Again

It turned out we only stayed in Crane about five months because Dad's job had been completed. Even though Dad knew the job was winding down, his boss didn't tell him where we would be moving next until the last day he worked in the munitions storage area. He came home and told us we would be moving back to Pennsylvania. And just like that, a couple of days later he was off to the new job.

It was time to repack all of our stuff. We had gained some furniture and bicycles, which meant we needed a bigger truck this time.

Moving this soon was sad. I really liked living in this new, modern house with the indoor plumbing and electric stove. The truck arrived, we loaded up and headed east again. This time we all rode in the car. It was late when we started making turns and moving slower. I had been sleeping for some time. I looked around and things started to look familiar.

I couldn't believe it. I knew where we were! My gosh, the street we turned down was the same street we had lived on in Moon Run. Then we pulled up to our old house. I sat up straight, wide awake. Did Sonny and Dolly still live next door? Would we be going back to the same school? I hoped it was true! We wouldn't have to find new friends. *Moon Run...we have friends here.* We were back!

Joan said, "This is great! No more being teased!"

On the front porch of our house in Crane.
RoseMary (10), Pat (12), Romaine (4), Ann (1),
John (6), Joan (9). September 1943

MOON RUN, PENNSYLVANIA II
January 1944

16. Back in Moon Run

I was looking forward to living in Moon Run again. I wondered if Dolly would want to be my friend any more. She acted so strange when we were leaving; just like she didn't care that we were going away forever. Well, if that was the way she felt I could always be friends with Judy. Judy lived a long way from us, but I knew she would be happy to see me.

It was past bedtime when we pulled into the parking spot by our old house. All of us kids went in and got our beds set up, then went to bed while the adults finished up unloading the truck. It felt so good just to lie down and not be cramped into a car full of people.

When I woke up in the morning the first thing I heard was someone knocking at the door. When Mom opened the door I heard Dolly say, "Are you all moved back? Are you going to live here again? Where are the kids?"

Mom answered, "Yes, yes and they are all still

asleep. They were so tired from the long trip."

"Oh, I'm so glad you've come back. We missed everyone so much. I cried for two days after you moved away," Dolly said.

"We're so happy to be here," Mom said. "We missed you all, too. How's your mom? Is she busy today?"

I was so glad to hear Dolly's voice, I just laid there and listened. Then I jumped out of bed and ran into the kitchen so we could hug each other. I had missed Dolly, too. We just stood there grinning at each other for a minute. Then we were both talking at once.

"Guess what? Aunt Millie is going to fix my hair today. I know she'll be wanting to fix yours, too. Can you come with me? Please let her come, Mrs. Quinn. It will be just like old times. Mrs. Quinn, can she come?" Dolly begged.

"I guess, just this once, but she has to unpack and put her things away when you get back," Mom answered.

We headed off to Aunt Millie's house. Dolly's Aunt Millie worked as a beauty operator. She would fix Dolly's and my hair once a week, just like we were grown-ups. Aunt Millie wasn't married. Neither was her sister, Laura, who lived with her. They were Mr. Mahoney's sisters and they felt bad whenever he went on a drinking binge. I think they wanted Dolly to have things he never had money to buy because of his drinking.

Aunt Millie set our hair with bobby pins and combed it into special grown-up styles that we were so proud to show off. We looked like what we were: not yet teenagers, with grandma hairstyles. Dolly's aunts also gave us their odds and ends of makeup, which we happily used. Sitting in front of the mirror in Mrs. Mahoney's bedroom, we made ourselves up to look like a couple of floozies in a 1920's movie.

Pat and Sonny laughed and teased us, but we were having too much fun to care. Mom and Mrs. Mahoney tried to tell us to use less makeup, but we never listened. It was a good thing we didn't live close enough to Aunt Millie for any of our other friends to see us all made up. When it came time to play games with the boys, we went as we were. But when it was time to go home, we always washed up first.

Dolly Mahoney with her hair all done.
Moon Run 1946

17. Measles

What a wonderful thing, to be back in Moon Run. I think Joan was the happiest of all. She knew everyone, so no one would tease her about her eyes and those thick glasses of hers. Dad and Mom took her to an eye doctor in Pittsburgh when we lived here before, so now they could take her back there again. They had found a specialist who was really helping her.

The rest of us were so thankful we didn't have to meet a whole new group of people. I guess we didn't care that we had to use an outhouse again. We also had to get our water from the pump. It was like a dream going back to a semi-primitive life with the kids whose fathers were coal miners. Coal mining was a very hard life, with not many benefits back in the 1940's. I couldn't believe the conditions they worked in. I heard some of the dads talking about the dust, the dark, the long hours and never getting out of debt because of the low pay. I was glad Dad had a much better job. We never seemed to have a money problem. Maybe it was because Mom and Dad never talked about money when we were around.

I was happy to be back in my old classes in school. I was doing even better than before. Then one day I went to school not feeling good. About the middle of my English class the teacher came over to me. She took me by the hand and led me out of the room. When we got in the hall she said, "How do you feel? You look sick. I think you have the measles."

"I feel kind of dizzy," I said. "I didn't feel too bad when I came in this morning, but I'm kind of sick now."

"I'm taking you to the principal's office to get you away from the rest of the class," she said. "Can anyone come get you?"

"No one can come. Dad has the car at work and he's fifteen miles away," I replied. "And besides, my mom doesn't know how to drive."

"Well, we'll have to figure something out," she said. "You can't come back to class."

They decided to have me sit in the principal's office until it was time to get the school bus for home. By that time, I felt much worse. It's hard to believe we didn't have cell phones back then. No television, no computer, no CD player, no iPad, no video games; they hadn't been invented.

I suffered through the bus ride home and spent the next ten days in bed. I was too sick to even get up to eat. I don't remember if anyone else got the measles, but I sure was sick enough for everyone. I finally got better and things settled down into a normal routine for the school year.

18. If We Only Had a Rope

One Saturday, Pat and Sonny were sitting on the edge of the porch looking across the valley trying to decide if they should venture over there. It was a lazy day when they didn't have anything special to do.

"We were playing by the slag heaps yesterday," Sonny said.

"That's okay. I'm tired of being so dirty," Pat said. "Mom told me I'd have to wash my own clothes if I did it again."

"It's bad enough we have to pump the water. Dolly ripped a sheet when she was putting it through the wringer in the washer. I don't want to get my fingers caught in that contraption," Sonny replied. "Men don't wash clothes anyway."

"I can see me now, telling Mom I'm not going to do something she told me to do," Pat said. "Dad would tan my hide if I tried that. We need to think of something to do."

They sat there being glum, just wishing someone would get an idea. Then Romaine and Joan came by, playing with a short rope. Joan wanted to jump rope and Romaine wanted to pretend he was a cowboy trying to lasso Susie, our dog.

"If we had a longer rope we could do all kinds of things," Pat said.

"The only rope my mom has is her clothes line," said Sonny.

"That's a great idea," said Pat. "My mom has one, too. She has it on the posts right now, but she isn't washing clothes today. I'll go see if we can use it."

Pat disappeared into the house looking for Mom, but she wasn't there. Then he remembered that Mom and Mrs. Mahoney had gone to see a friend who was sick. They were going to do some house cleaning for her.

Back outside, the boys decided to go see if they could take the clothesline off the posts so they could play with it. One end was easy to get down, but Dad had wired the other end to the post so it wouldn't come untied when clothes were hanging there.

"Just our luck. What can a guy do with a rope tied to a post?" said Pat. "Seems we're not going to use the dang thing." Then he had an inspiration. "What if we pretend we're doing that track stuff? You know, like we saw last week at the movie."

"You mean the high jump?" asked Sonny. "Sure, we can tie the other end to that fence post to make it lower. I saw some kids at the high school jumping over a stick two others were holding. He could get really high."

"Sounds good to me. Let's try it with the rope tied since we don't have anyone to hold it," said Pat.

They started low, and jumped over it. They raised the rope several times and finally couldn't get over it. They jumped a few more times and then were bored again.

"I've got another idea," said Pat. "I'll be right back." He ran around to the kitchen door and inside. He found the broom and mop handle. He took the rags Mom scrubbed the floor with off the mop handle and ran back to where Sonny was waiting.

"Look what I brought. Now we can pole vault and get even higher," Pat said with a wide smile.

The boys adjusted the rope to where they could practice getting over it with their makeshift poles.

"This works! Why didn't we think of this sooner?" Sonny said. "Let's see how high we can get."

Several jumps later and the broom showed signs of excessive wear. The mop handle had lost part of the clamp that kept the rags in place. Oh well, they figured they would just fix it when they put it away. About that time Romaine and John showed up. They made a good audience clapping and cheering for every jump. When Joan showed up, she stood there shaking her head.

"You're going to get it when Mom sees her broom. It won't sweep anymore," she said.

"You better not tell or I'll beat you up," Pat said. "Just go away. We're having fun."

It was too late. Mom and Mrs. Mahoney walked around the corner just in time to see Sonny run and vault over the rope with Mom's broom in hand.

"What's going on here? Just look at my broom." Mom held up the broom for us all to see. "I guess I know who'll be sweeping until I get a new broom. I see my mop handle is missing a part, too. You will be scrubbing on your hands and knees for a while, Henry Patrick." We knew he was in serious trouble when Mom used Pat's real name.

Mrs. Mahoney informed Sonny he would be helping. "Get ready to be his helper. Did you take any of my stuff?"

Sonny shook his head, *no.*

"I think it's time to start working," she said.

The boys were still down on their hands and knees scrubbing the kitchen when Dad got home from work that night. Mom showed him the broom. I saw Dad grinning when he looked at it.

"Boys, if you don't think before you do something, you have to think while you're paying the price for your mistake. The floor looks pretty good." Dad walked away with a big smile on his face. I bet he was remembering a time when he had been punished for having fun with things he shouldn't have been using.

19. Profanity

One Saturday, we were playing nothing in particular in the yard. I was thinking it was a warm day for early April – it was much warmer in Moon Run than in northern Minnesota. Seven-year-old John got a little hot headed and said a few too many forbidden words. We were used to hearing him spout off and ignored him. What John didn't know was that Dad had just stepped onto the porch and heard the whole thing.

"Kids, get over here. I want to talk to you," Dad yelled so we all could hear. We all lined up in front of the porch. We stood there waiting while Dad looked us over deciding what to say. I stood on one foot and then the other, knowing swearing was something Dad particularly frowned upon. Dad looked us over and waited. I hated waiting. It made me feel guilty even when I was innocent.

"I guess we all have something to talk about just now. I heard John say a few choice words, words no one says around here. Now I want to know, who taught him those words?" Dad had a serious look on his face.

He looked us over again and waited for an answer. We were all squirming and standing there nervously when Mom came out the door. She stood on the porch waiting for someone to start talking.

"Was it you?" he asked Pat. Pat shrugged his shoulders.

"Was it you?" he said, looking at me. I shook my head, staring at the ground.

"Was it you, Joan?"

"Not me. I hit. Kids laugh when I beat up someone. I don't swear," Joan answered in a matter of fact tone.

"Well, since no one will admit it, I'll ask John. What do you say, John? Who taught you that bad language?"

John just stood there for a minute looking everyone over. Dad gave him a look that said, *I'm waiting*, and folded his arms. John took a deep breath, looking like he was ready to confess.

"Mom taught me," John said, dead serious.

If he had said Mom's sister, Aunt Margaret, no one would have thought anything about it, but Mom? Mom got a horrified look on her face, turned on her heel, and went into the house. I had never ever heard Mom yell, let alone swear. Dad's face was frozen in disbelief. He turned and walked away. He took a couple of minutes and went back in the house. Mom was busy at the stove, cooking lunch for us. She did a lot of stirring and stayed busy.

"I'd like to know. When did you take up cussing?" Dad asked with a chuckle. "That boy's lying is getting out of control. What do you think we should do?"

Mom turned around slowly and said to Dad, "Al,

what are we going to do with him? I never know when
he's truthful. I'm so at a loss I don't know what to do
with him."

"Well, I've been thinking about that and I am also
at a loss. For some reason he seems to believe what he
says. I have to figure out a way to make him realize
what an awful thing being called a liar is. I'm going to
go out there and make him give you an apology he'll
never forget."

Dad walked back out the door. "Kids, come over
here and line up for me. I talked to Mom and she is
sitting by the table crying. Her heart is broken. She
never thought you'd discover that she lies. She wants
you all to come in the house so she can apologize and
promise to never lie again."

We all went in the house. I had never thought Mom
lied. We all stood there in the kitchen watching Mom
sit there crying. We were all crying now, too. We didn't
know what to do to get her to stop crying.

Dad questioned, "Is there anyone here who can tell
me how to get Mom to stop crying?"

We looked at each other wondering what we could
do. Ann went and crawled onto Mom's lap and Mom
cried louder.

Then Joan said, "I never heard Mom lie. Mom,
please don't lie." She walked over and stood by Mom.

Romaine followed her and sat down on a chair. He
sat there staring at John. I gave John a shove.

"I know Mom never cussed in front of us. I know
Mom never taught John to cuss," I told everyone, not
able to control my tears.

Dad never said a word, just stood there looking at
Mom. That's when Pat went over and stood by Dad. We
all stared at John. We waited and waited. After what
seemed like forever, John got tears on his cheeks.

He went over and hugged Mom. John said over and over again, "I'm sorry, Mom, so sorry." We all turned and started to walk away to let Mom sort it out with John.

I sure hoped that John meant what he said and that he was truly sorry. I never wanted to see Mom cry again. For Mom and Dad, it was over. The subject never came up again.

20. Bath Time

Saturday afternoon was bath time for us. One Saturday Mom walked out onto the porch and said, "Pat, John, come here. I need water."

She turned and reentered the kitchen. It was already four o'clock and it would take at least half an hour for the water to be hot enough for baths. She didn't know how it had gotten so late, but it would be a rush to get everyone in and out of the tub and still have supper ready by the time Dad got home from work.

Life can sure be strange sometimes. Less than a month ago back in Indiana, we had every convenience you could imagine. Here in Moon Run, we didn't even have running water. What Mom missed most, though, was having a bathroom. A bathtub was a true sign of being modern. Here she was, about to get us kids in and out of a washtub. All of us had to bathe in the same water. The one big room that was our kitchen, dining room and living room, was not Mom's idea of fine living. But, living without Dad was out of the question. She was willing to put up with bad living conditions as long as we could all be together.

The boys came in to get the buckets so they could fill them with water. John said, "Why do we have to take baths today? We didn't do anything to get dirty."

Mom said, "I can see that you are clean, but Dad has better eyesight than I do. You'll just have to get in the washtub and scrub up so Dad won't be upset because I didn't make you take a bath. Hop to it. You'll have to bathe in cold water if we don't get it on the stove."

I helped Mom stoke up the coal stove so the fire would be hot enough to heat the water quickly. I had finally learned how to lift the lid so as not to let the smelly coal smoke out into the room – it was so simple; just open the damper. My next job was to convince Mom that I should be the first one in the tub. I hated taking a bath after the other kids. The water would be cold by then and they were dirtier than me – I really didn't like it if I got dirty.

Joan didn't care if she took a bath after everybody else. Maybe it was because of her bad eyesight. Without her glasses she could hardly see anything, let alone dirt. The boys thought the dirtier they got the more it was a sign that they could do man stuff. Dad always came home dirty because he spent his whole day moving dirt. If anything went wrong at work, he had to help the mechanic fix the bulldozer and he'd be covered with grease. We kids got our baths on Saturday. Dad got one every day. Mom said it was easier for him to have a bath than for her to wash the sheets every day.

Joan and I got to take our baths first. John was complaining to Pat, "We had to get the water, how come the girls are taking baths while we wait outside?"

Pat said, "I like to be last. It's hard to stay clean until after church tomorrow. Don't be dumb. What do you have to do after you get a bath? Stay clean. No more fun. Would we be here playing marbles if we already had our baths?"

There was no way they could stay clean on their knees in the sand. Pat was right, the later the bath, the less time they had to sit around staying clean.

In those days there was no Saturday night Mass. It was on Sunday morning and we had better still be clean. Going to church dirty was a sin in Mom and Dad's eyes. After church every Sunday we all hurried to change our clothes so we could get back to being ourselves.

This was our regular routine on the weekends back in the 1940's. Even though we had our bath on Saturday, we did have to wash our face, hands and feet in a basin at bedtime every night. It took about the same time as taking a bath but it sure seemed a lot easier.

Dad with Pat (13) on Pat's Confirmation day.
Moon Run, PA, April 1944

21. Being a Tomboy

In Moon Run, girls did girl things and played girl games. Back in Markville, boys and girls all played together. I guess if we wanted a team of anything, we had no choice. There just weren't enough of us.

I was always bugging the boys in Moon Run to let me play with them. I never got to unless they really needed another player. One day the boys were playing in the field above our house. That field was our best playground for all of our games. I was tired of girl games and decided to see what the boys were playing. I went to the field and watched them playing football.

There were only five boys there, making it hard to do much. I stood there watching and saw the boys struggling to get anywhere. Then one boy started whispering to another as he was looking my way.

Sonny came over and said, "If you won't be a pain and act like a girl you can play with us."

"I never play like a girl. What do you want me to do?" I said, looking forward to finally playing with the boys.

"Come over and we'll show you."

I followed him over where the other boys were standing and waited for one of them to tell me. They whispered among themselves for a minute and sent Pat over to tell me their rules.

Pat said, "Don't be stupid. Just play like we did in Markville. I told them you could run fast and never cried if you got hurt. So don't cry. You're on my side. Let's go."

We played cautiously for a few plays and the boys never let me touch the football. Then the other team got the ball. We were playing touch football, so the fastest runners had the best team. A time or two the ball changed from their team to our team, then they had the ball again.

We were all running as fast as we could but they were getting close to a touchdown. I was closest to the boy with the ball, and he was headed for a touchdown. I ran after him and was gaining ground but the goal line was so close the only way I could catch him was to dive at him.

I dived as far as I could and grabbed for his feet. My hands touched his legs, preventing the touchdown, but the heal of his left shoe caught me right in the teeth. I let go of his leg and rolled over on my side. My mouth was bleeding and my head was spinning. The next thing I knew; all the boys were standing there looking down at me.

"Are you dead?" I heard one of them ask. "Are we in trouble because she's hurt? Will she tell your mom?"

"She better not," I heard Pat say.

"Well, she wanted to play. It's her fault," Sonny said.

I sat up, looked at them and said, "I won't tell any-

81

one I got hurt."

My mouth hurt really bad. I could feel that my two front teeth were loose. Now I wanted to cry. My tears were ready to fall, but somehow I held them back. I got up and walked around. I was not going to quit. They would never let me play again if I quit, and I wasn't about to let that happen.

We started lining up to play again. I wanted to go get a rag to wipe my mouth and face. I knew if I got hit again I would cry.

Just then I heard Sonny's mom call for him to come home. Everyone stopped and looked at him.

"I got to go," he kind of whispered.

We all headed off of the field. Pat came over to walk by me.

"You did good," he said. "Are you going to tell Mom? Dad better not find out. He'll never let us play again."

"I won't tell. You go get me a wet rag so I can clean my face."

We walked to the back of the house where Pat snuck in to get a rag. We went up by the pump and got some water to wash my face. My lip didn't swell because it didn't get kicked. Somehow, Mom never noticed anything.

I ate carefully until my teeth weren't loose any more. I played with the boys after that, but never made the mistake of trying to tackle again. If you want to play by their rules, the first rule is, *no crying.*

22. John's High School Friends

The high school was just across the road from the elementary school in Moon Run so it was easy for all of us students to see what was going on "across the road." Of course, the elementary kids were far more fascinated by what was happening at the high school.

One day Julie, one of Pat's classmates, asked Pat, "How come your brother John is always going over to the high school?"

Pat answered, "How would I know? It wasn't my day to watch him."

"I saw him go over there twice last week," Julie said. "They have lunch at the same time we do. He went with some other kid again today."

"Is he still over there," Pat asked.

"I don't know. I was playing on the swings and didn't watch for him," she answered.

"There goes the bell. It's time to go back to class," said Pat. "If he's still there the teacher will find out what he's up to."

When they got on the school bus to go home Pat looked for John. He was sitting in the back of the bus talking to a girl. Home was only two stops away, so Pat decided to stay where he was. He'd ask John what he was up to when they got off the bus.

As soon as they got off the bus John ran down the hill to go home as fast as he could. Pat looked for him but John must have guessed that Pat was ready to question him and he didn't want to tell.

Pat waited for lunch hour the next day and ran across the street to find out what had John so interested in crossing the road. He wandered around to the back of the high school looking for John. As he turned the corner he saw several high school boys leaning against the building, smoking cigarettes. Right in among the group stood John. It was no surprise to Pat that John had a cigarette in his hand.

Pat stood there trying to decide who to yell at first. It had to be the big boys since they were the ones sharing their cigarettes with John. Pat waded right in to the middle of the group, saying, "What are you doing, giving this little kid cigarettes? I can't wait to point you out to the principal for smoking on school grounds; even worse, giving a second grader cigarettes."

They all had their eyes on Pat, then one of the boys said, "He said he's a midget. We thought he was a junior in the Special Ed class. John, how could you lie to us like that?"

John stood there with a dumb look on his face. Pat knew he was thinking up a lie. He couldn't wait to find out how he would explain this one.

"They asked me if I was sixteen and had I ever smoked before so I said yes," John blurted out. "I meant yes, I had smoked before."

"You know, lying is a sin," Pat scolded. "You make up all sorts of excuses and do whatever you please! I guess you can explain this to Dad when he gets home from work tonight."

John blurted out, "I didn't lie! They knew I wasn't sixteen! They saw me come over from across the road. They were just being nice – please don't report them to the principal. It would be my fault if they got kicked out of school. They're my friends."

Pat just shook his head. "You have adult friends, but you fight with kids your age. I don't get it. Why can't you just get along with kids your own age?"

When Dad got home that night, Pat told him to ask John what he was doing at the high school. John fessed up and told Dad he had been smoking with some high school boys. Dad made him name every one of them. Then John got a long lecture about not smoking and not lying. For his punishment, Dad grounded John for a month and made him do extra chores around the house.

John sure knew how to get in trouble. He always had Joan fighting his battles and Romaine running to get her help. When he wasn't fighting he was figuring out other ways to get in trouble. We just never knew what it would be next.

23. Romaine's Adventure

School was out for the summer and now was the time to really explore. The hills around Moon Run were so tempting. Pat and Sonny had great tales to tell. They found trails that led them into the woods and caves with wooden KEEP OUT signs nailed to the entrance.

John wanted to go with them, but no, he was too slow or would tell Dad. Not that anything stopped John when he made up his mind. *Romaine won't care,* John thought. *He'll come anywhere I want him to go.*

"Romaine, let's have an adventure. Want to come?" John asked.

"What's an adventure?"

"It's something Pat and Sonny do when they go over the railroad track bed and up that hill over there," John said.

"Oh, I want to go but Pat says I'm too little. He just doesn't want to wait for me. I can go pretty fast, you know," Romaine said, feeling all grown up.

"I'll wait for you. When you get tired, we'll come home. Let's get a sandwich and eat it like a picnic when we get to our adventure," John said.

They made some sandwiches and headed down the hill to cross the old track bed. When they got to the trees going up the hill Romaine sat down on a fallen log, thinking, *I'm tired of carrying this sandwich. I'm hungry – it must be time to eat.*

"What are you doing?" asked John. "It's not time to eat. Come on!"

"My sandwich is getting too heavy," replied Romaine. "My stomach wants it." Romaine started eating his sandwich.

"Boy, I'm never going to bring you on an adventure if you get tired so quick," John scolded. "You're no fun. Joan would be better than you."

"That sandwich was good," said Romaine. "Okay, let's go. Where are we going?"

"I think we can find stuff to do when we go up there," John said, pointing up the hill toward the abandoned coal mine Pat and Sonny had told him about when they came home after spending time searching the woods.

They climbed higher and still Romaine complained. John soon tired of all the complaining.

"That's it! We're going back. The next adventure I take, you have to stay home," John said.

"You make me come when I'm hungry. I'd be fine if you'd let me have more food," Romaine snapped back.

The two of them argued all the way home. John decided it would be a lot more fun with Joan, even if she was just a girl.

24. Playing Girl Games

One Saturday we were finishing up our chores before we could go play. Joan was sweeping the big bedroom and I was putting dishes away into the dynamite box cupboards in the kitchen. Of course, the boys were already playing outside. They didn't have as many chores as we did because, as they quickly reminded us, "Girls do all the housework chores, and boys work outside." As sickening as it was to Joan and me, there were more girl's chores than boy's chores. This was something Joan and I complained about every Saturday.

We were hurrying to get outside to play with the boys when the phone rang.

Mom answered, "Hello. Yes, really? Come on over. The kids will have fun."

Then Mom yelled to Dad, "Al, Sylvia and Al are on their way over."

Dad yelled back, "Good, Big Al mentioned they wanted to go shopping today."

Dad called Uncle Albert *Big Al* or *Big Brother Al* because he was seven minutes older than Dad. They spent a lot of time explaining they were twins because they didn't look it. Some people even doubted they were brothers, they were so different from each other in looks and size.

Mom turned to talk to Joan and me. "Girls, Maxine and Judy will be here this afternoon to play."

"Good," I said happily. "We won't have to play with the boys." I loved when my cousins came over.

"About that," Mom said. "I want you to play girl games. You know Maxine and Judy will be wearing some of their good clothes, so no climbing trees or playing in the swamp. They'll be in big trouble if you talk them into playing where they'll get dirty or wet and muddy."

"How come they can't come in their old clothes?" Joan asked. "It's no fun just sitting around pretending to have fun." Joan had a way of stating things in a matter of fact fashion.

Mom was stern, "You stop complaining and get finished with your chores! They'll be here soon. They may not be here very long. I don't know what kind of shopping Uncle Albert and Aunt Sylvia are doing."

After we finished our chores, we went out to sit on the porch while we waited for them to come. Joan, who thought keeping clean was for everybody else, could get dirty just sitting on the porch. It wasn't long before Uncle Albert drove up to the house. He began his routine of getting the car parked and ready for the next trip. We all said hello for a few minutes and then it was time for Uncle Albert and Aunt Sylvia to go shopping. Mom and Dad went back in the house.

We four girls stood around deciding what we could do while staying clean. Our options were: go for a walk, play hop scotch, go for a walk, play beauty shop, or go for a walk. We were limited on what we could do without getting dirty and none of them sounded very fun at the time.

Judy piped up, "I don't care. I want to play tag. I can run fast and I'm never *it*. The boys always get mad because they can't catch me. Let's tell the boys we want to play tag."

"Last time we played tag you tore your dress," Maxine replied. "We better not play tag today."

While Maxine and Judy argued back and forth, the boys stopped playing army and came over to see what we were doing.

Pat asked, "What are you girls going to do, just stand there and wait for us to ask you to play?"

"We have lots of ideas! We can play without you!" I shot back.

"I bet you just want us to ask you to play," Donnie said. "You never have ideas of your own." I know he was trying to sound like the boys didn't want to play with us.

We all stood around some more and no new play ideas surfaced. The boys started walking away.

"I want to play tag," Judy said, not wanting to miss the opportunity.

Joan agreed, "Me too. It's more fun when lots of people play."

The two of them walked over by the boys, who were doing, *Eeny, meeny, miny, moe,* to see who would be it.

"Well, Mom will be so upset if she gets dirty or rips her dress," said Maxine. "I don't care if she gets in trouble – I'm not getting dirty."

"Me neither," I said. "The boys make up new rules and cheat. It's no fun getting beat by them, especially when they cheat."

We walked toward the road to go for a walk, feeling superior to the other kids. Maybe we would run into some other girls, then we could play our own game. After walking for a little while, we could hear how much fun the kids were having back at the house. Since we hadn't found anyone else to play with, we turned around and went back to play tag with them.

After a while, Maxine, Judy, Joan and I decided to do something else. We crossed over the railroad track bed, through the field beyond and into the blackberry patch. Bears like blackberries and we liked worrying if a bear would show up. We didn't take any containers along for the berries, so we ate everything we picked. As usually happens when you pick blackberries, we got the juice all over our fingers and faces.

Without thinking, Judy wiped her face on her sleeve, then her hands on the skirt of her pretty green dress. "Oh, no!" she said. "My dress is stained!"

"Now, you did it," Maxine said. "Mom's going to yell at you. It's not my fault you ruined your dress."

"She didn't ruin her dress," I said. "We'll wash it at the pump."

"Mom will find out," Maxine said doubtfully. "She sees everything. I didn't want to go berry picking anyway. We better hurry so your dress can dry out before they get here."

"This isn't my best dress. Maybe Mom won't get upset," Judy said, trying not to cry. She knew her dress was a mess.

We headed home to see if we could save the day. The pump was at the top of the hill by our house.

"We better hurry," Judy said. "If they see us trying to wash out the blackberry stains, Dad will make me sit in the car until we go home. Maybe you could get some soap. Do you think soap will take out the stains?"

Joan and I looked at each other to decide who should go for soap.

"Joan, you get some soap. I can pump water better than you can," I ordered.

"I can pump water, too," Joan said.

"You always need help," I said. "We don't want the boys to know. They would blab, especially Romaine. He is the biggest blabbermouth of them all."

"Please, get some soap," Judy pleaded. "My dress needs to dry before Mom and Dad get back. Will Aunt Hildegard tell if she finds out?"

We were still trying to get the stains out when the boys showed up. They weren't any help at all, just commenting on how much trouble Judy was in. Then Judy started to cry. Judy hardly ever cried, but she was scared to have her mom know. Aunt Sylvia was a very nice lady, but she wanted her girls to be clean at all times.

"Pat, help pump water," I said. "We all have fun when our cousins come over. Judy just made a mistake and we want to fix it."

We continued scrubbing on Judy's dress, to no avail.

"Look, the soap isn't helping," I said. "Mom uses bleach to take stains out of stuff. I'll go get some bleach to see if that works."

I ran to the house and brought back the bottle of bleach, making sure Mom didn't see me. Joan helped Judy hold her skirt out so I could pour the bleach onto the stain. I began to pour the bleach directly onto her dress. It only took a second to realize there was now a huge, ugly whitish yellow spot on her dress where I had poured the bleach. Not only did the bleach take out the blackberry stain, it had also taken out all of the pretty green color!

"Uh-oh, we're all in trouble!" I gasped.

Before the words were out of my mouth, all of the other kids ran away. Judy and I were left standing there with the incriminating evidence plain as day right on the front of Judy's dress. We knew we had to be the ones to show Aunt Sylvia. We slowly walked to the house and sat on the porch waiting for our punishment.

It seemed like forever before Uncle Albert and Aunt Sylvia came back from shopping. When they drove up, they could immediately tell something was wrong.

Uncle Albert was out of the car first. He stood there just looking at us, waiting for Aunt Sylvia to get out of the car. She hesitated, then opened the car door and headed toward us.

Judy was crying, I was standing behind her and all the other kids were still in hiding.

Aunt Sylvia looked at Judy, looked at me, then looked back at Judy as she said, "What happened?"

All I could say was, "I'm sorry, I'm so sorry. We tried to fix it and all we did was make it worse."

By this time, Mom and Dad came out to see what was going on. After all the explaining was finished and Mom told Aunt Sylvia she didn't know I had taken the bleach, Aunt Sylvia very kindly said, "I made the girls wear dresses that they have outgrown just in case they couldn't resist getting dirty. It's a lesson for all. *Think before you do, and especially, ask about results when you're doing something you have no experience with.*"

I gained a heathy respect for bleach that day.

Maxine (age 6) and Judy (age 4) Quinn
Easter Sunday, 1943
Photo Courtesy Judy Quinn McConnell

25. Romaine and the Tomatoes

Some of us kids went apple picking and just got back with a couple of big bags of apples. Now Mom wanted help making apple sauce. At five, Romaine was too little to help peel the apples, so he just wandered around looking for something to do. He didn't have anyone to play with except Ann. Ann was only two, and for the most part he had to keep her from running off when she tried to leave the yard. That was a big job because we didn't have a fence.

Finally, it was time for Ann's nap and Romaine was really looking for something to do. Maybe he could go throw rocks at the outhouse. He threw one rock and *oops*, someone was in the outhouse. Someone started yelling so he started running. He didn't hit anyone and couldn't figure out why they were so mad. He ran around the house so he wouldn't get caught.

When he got on the road up next to where the Bauchkies lived, he sat down on their step. It was quiet.

The radio was usually loud, so he guessed no one was home. Mr. Bauchkie always listened to Polka music when he was home. When his son Leo was there, he turned it to Big Band music – he loved to dance. Anyway, it was quiet now.

Mr. Bauchkie's sixteen-year-old daughter, Julie, had tomatoes spread on the porch to ripen. He looked the tomatoes over and thought he'd eat one. *Julie is nice; she won't be mad,* he said to himself. He grabbed a nice juicy red one and ate it. *Mmm...that was good.* He looked the tomatoes over again. A bird had pecked on one of them and left a hole in it. Julie would probably throw that one away. He thought, *I can throw it away for her.*

He threw the bad tomato at a rock across the driveway. *Missed. I better try that again.* He picked up another tomato and threw it. *Missed again.*

I know I can hit that rock if I stand up. He threw another one. *Missed again. Well, maybe that rock is too far away.* The next time he chose a rock that was closer to the porch. He picked up another tomato and threw it. *I almost hit it! Well now, this must be the rock I was supposed to hit!* He picked up another tomato and threw it. *Yes! I hit it! I wonder if I can I do that again.*

He threw another tomato. *Got it!* Another tomato. *Missed.* Another tomato. *Missed.* Another tomato. *Got it! Just one more – I know I can get two in a row.* He threw his last one. *Got it! I knew I could do it!*

After that wonderful accomplishment he looked at the tomatoes on the porch. *Uh-oh, there are a lot of tomatoes gone. Julie is going to be mad.*

He started to panic. *What should I do? Maybe if I spread them out on the porch she won't notice any are missing.* He spread them all out. *Oh no, that is even worse.* He had an even better idea. *If I throw them all away maybe she will forget she even had any tomatoes on the porch at all! I better hurry; someone might come and catch me in the act.*

He started throwing tomatoes across the road as fast as he could. Some of them made it across the road, but most of them made a big mess in the middle of the road. *What a mess, I better run!*

Romaine ran back around the house and sat on the porch at home. He was safe. No one saw him. He sat there for a while and before long Pat came and sat beside him.

"Romaine, what were you doing?" Pat asked.

"Just playing," Romaine answered.

"Just playing, huh?" Pat asked. "What's that on your pants? Looks like you made a big mess someplace. Is that tomato on your pants?"

Romaine squirmed as he tried to make up an answer. Before he could figure out what to say, along came Julie around the corner. She was furious!

"Do you know what happened to my tomatoes?" she demanded.

Pat looked at Romaine, waiting for him to speak up. Not a sound did he make. Romaine squirmed again and looked away. Pat looked at Julie and shrugged his shoulders.

"All my tomatoes are gone," said Julie. "The road is a mess. Whoever did it just threw them out in the road. Why would anyone do that? Not one tomato left on the porch!" She turned and walked back around the house, tears on her cheeks.

Pat shook his head. "Romaine, you better hide. This is big trouble. I'm sure glad you did it, not me."

When Dad got home that night the whole story came out. Dad marched Romaine up to tell Julie the tomatoes would be replaced. Then Dad made Romaine tell Julie he was sorry and that he would never do anything like that again. Next, Romaine had to clean up the road. Then he had to ask Julie if there was anything else he could do to prove that he was sorry.

It took a while before he finished the chores Julie asked him to do, but Romaine lived through it and learned his lesson.

26. On to Clymer

Not long after Romaine's episode with the toma-toes, Dad came home from work and said, "Kids, I hope you're ready for another adventure because my company is moving my job again. We're moving to Clymer, Pennsylvania. Time to pack 'em up and move 'em out."

I couldn't believe my ears. We had only been back in Moon Run for the rest of the school year and now we had to move again. This sure was a new way of life. All of us kids groaned when we heard the news, but we knew we never wanted to be without Dad.

Once again, we packed up the moving truck and said good-bye to our good friends in Moon Run, not knowing if we would ever see them again.

Clymer is about sixty miles or so east of Pittsburgh. We couldn't have lived there more than two months because we never entered school there. This was the summer of 1944.

CLYMER, PENNSYLVANIA
July 1944

27. Railroad Bridge

One Saturday not long after we moved to Clymer, John and Romaine were playing with some kids who were bragging about all the stuff they did after they were told, "Never do that." Even at age seven, John was one of those kids who believed there was not a thing he couldn't do.

There was a boy named Bolder who was telling all the kids how brave he had been. Yes, indeed, he was the bravest one of all.

Bolder said, "Just let me tell you how I crossed the river on the railroad bridge. I didn't walk on the ties and rails. No sir, I went under all that. I crawled on the bridging. It took a long time because there is no straight way to just go across. The bridging is all criss-crossed under there. Some beams go up while other beams go down. It took a long time. No one else here ever did it."

He rattled along describing how dangerous it was and how lucky he was to make it.

"When a train goes over the bridge, the whole things shakes," he said.

John was completely taken in. He knew he could do it and wanted to show everyone who was the bravest of all the kids. When the group broke up to go do something else, John and Romaine headed toward the river so they could get a better look at the bridge.

"Look how easy it will be," John said. "It's not that far. We can cross over and back before it's time for supper. Come on, Romaine, now's the time."

"It doesn't sound like fun to me. I think we can wait until tomorrow." Romaine said. He was scared.

"It could be raining tomorrow. I think the trains are done for today," John said as he hurried toward the bridge.

Romaine was straggling behind. With every step he took he was more convinced this was a bad idea. He was pretty short to reach those beams. What if he got stranded out there? He didn't want to fall in the water.

John yelled at Romaine, "Will you hurry? We don't want a train to come while we're crossing the bridge."

"I changed my mind," Romaine yelled back. "I'm not coming. I'm too short to reach those cross bars. Go without me – you'll go faster." Then Romaine said to himself, *John thinks I can do everything.*

"Okay, but stay here and watch," John said. "I want people to believe me when I tell them that I did it."

Off he went, deciding where to start. One look back and John could see that Romaine was headed for home.

Romaine rounded the corner to see Joan playing by herself in front of the porch.

"You'll never guess what John's doing right now," he said to her.

"I don't want to know," Joan replied. "He's the biggest know-it-all. Besides, I can do anything he can do."

"You're just mad because I was there and you weren't," Romaine said. "I watched him when he climbed up on the bridging. I saw him get on the beam..."

Before Romaine could finish his sentence Dad called, "Joan! John! Where are you?" Just then he saw Joan and Romaine over by the car. "What are you two doing?" He walked over to them and stood waiting for an answer. "I see you two are here, but where's John?"

Romaine looked up at Dad and said, "He's over on the railroad bridge."

"What is he doing by the bridge?" Dad asked.

"He's going over it."

"Well, who's with him?" Dad asked with a little panic in his voice.

Romaine answered, "Nobody. He wanted me to go but I said no. I'm too short to reach those cross braces. Besides, I didn't want to get into trouble."

Now there was anger in Dad's voice. "That kid! I'll...I'll...Oh, never mind." Then he took off toward the bridge with several of us kids following him.

Meanwhile, John was slowly working himself out to the middle of the river. He stopped to listen to see if he could hear a train coming. He thought, *No, not yet. I better hurry. It's taking a lot longer than I thought it would. Boy, I hope I make it before a train gets here. I don't want to look down. I didn't know it was so high. I wonder how deep the water is.*

At last, John reached the other side of the river. He tried to figure out how to get out from under the bridge. There was no way he wanted to go back the same way – that was way too hard. He sat down to rest for a moment, happy that he had made it in one piece.

Then he crawled out from under the tracks and heard, "Hello, John." Uh-oh, that was Dad's voice across the river.

"Would you like to tell me what a seven-year-old is doing on the railroad bridge?" Dad sounded really mad.

"I just thought it would be fun," John said with no remorse whatsoever.

"Was it?" Dad asked, trying to hold back his anger.

"Not really," John said. "It took longer than I thought. But now I can tell the other kids about it."

I don't know if I've ever seen Dad so mad at one of us kids. He started to yell at John across the river.

"Number One: you are not to tell anyone you did this."

"Number Two: you will never cross this bridge again after you come back."

"Number Three: if you see any other kid trying to cross this bridge you will tell an adult IMMEDIATELY. Do you understand?"

John yelled back, "Yes, Dad."

Dad continued, "It's not smart or brave. This bridge is at least twenty feet above the water. Kids aren't supposed to die. Now get yourself back over here the same way you got over there."

Now Dad's voice was more calm and steady. "I'll be watching so take your time. And DO NOT FALL."

John slowly made his way back over the river, concentrating on every move. I believe he realized how dangerous it was to be on the bridge even when a train wasn't crossing over it. Dad gave John a nice, long lecture all the way home. We were all happy that he didn't fall in the river. John had to promise Dad he would never try anything like that again.

28. Suppertime

Suppertime was the best meal for us. It was always the same every day – we ate as a family at the table. We were never called to supper; we just showed up. Dad trained us to show up. When the other kids headed home for supper we headed home, too. Another reason was because of our plates.

If we came home late for supper Dad turned our plate upside down. Have you ever seen that small circle on the bottom of your plate? It sure doesn't hold very much food and we weren't allowed to have seconds if we came home late. What if we were having soup? We didn't get much at all to eat that night. If we didn't get home during dinner it was worse.

The plate stayed there, upside down, until supper. When supper was finished the plate went back on the stack of plates on the shelf. No plate; no supper. It was a long time until breakfast. I was only late one time and I learned my lesson. I didn't like going hungry!

When we were all home for supper it was sure to be

fun because Dad always had a story to tell. One time Dad said, "Do you kids know your mom is Dutch?"

We all looked at her as she said, "No I am not. You all know that we are German."

Mom never spoke English until she started school. She hated not being able to talk to the other kids in school. She told us it was because her dad, Grandpa Libel, couldn't speak English when he got here from Germany. He never really spoke English because all the people in the area spoke German. Grandpa would come to visit us in Markville and he always spoke German even though Mom told him he was supposed to speak English to us. Mom wouldn't let us learn German – she never wanted us to be teased like she was as a child.

"Yes, she is Dutch," Dad said with a grin. "Do you know she was wearing wooden shoes when we met?"

Romaine asked, "Wooden shoes? How could you walk in wooden shoes?"

"Al, would you please tell them the truth?" Mom asked with a strain in her voice. "You know I only wore wooden shoes to the barn."

Dad kept going. "Okay, listen to this, kids. The first time I saw Mom she was just finishing up her chores in the barn. Leather shoes were expensive and got ruined if you wore them to the barn. The manure and animal urine would soak into the stitching and take the polish off the leather. That made your shoes look old and smell stinky. Grandpa Libel only had girls for help. They hated when their shoes smelled and tried not to go to the barn in their good shoes. Grandpa solved the problem by getting them wooden shoes just like he wore in the Old Country before he came to America."

"The shoes were easy to wash and they weren't so

bad to wear just to the barn," Mom explained.

"What a fib," Dad said with a laugh. "You should have been there on our wedding day. I had to take Mom down and sit on her to get those clod-hoppers off her feet."

We all laughed to think of Dad pulling those shoes off Mom. I couldn't imagine how she kept them on her feet. They didn't have laces or buckles. If I didn't tie my laces my shoes fell off when I ran.

Now Mom was getting upset, but Dad just grinned.

"Al, you know that's not true," she said. "I never wore them away from the barn. That was it." Mom knew we didn't believe him, but he never got tired of telling us that story.

"Just a minute. Let's get back to you being Dutch." Dad was not going to let go of this story. "How come your dad had that saying about being Dutch? When we moved to Markville, it was full of loggers. A good share of them were Swedish. When Grandpa came to visit and you kids got into fights outside, do you remember what he always said?"

We looked at each other, shrugging our shoulders. Not even Pat remembered what the saying was. Mom just sighed and walked into the kitchen.

Dad laughed, "Okay, does anyone remember what Grandpa said?"

"Don't believe a word of it. Your dad likes to tell stories," Mom yelled from the kitchen.

"The Irish and the Dutch, they don't amount to much, BUT they can lick the Swedes." Dad had a huge smile on his face, thoroughly enjoying telling the story.

"How do we know if we're fighting with the Swedes?" John asked.

"John, with your very blonde hair and blue eyes, you can fight with everyone you want to swing at. No one will care if you're Irish or a Swede," Dad said with a laugh.

We all laughed. We knew John liked to fight for no reason at all.

Dad also liked to tell us about how he would take Mom dancing. "I loved to dance. I'd get Mom out on the dance floor but she wasn't into dancing; but that only slowed me down a little."

Dad grabbed Mom right there and tried to get her to dance in the kitchen. She protested.

Then Dad said, "Just like when we were young. I'd get Mom on the dance floor. She'd stand there and I'd dance around her. She always did the same non-dance. It could be a Polka, Waltz or Schottische; she'd let me dance around her. The other girls would flirt with me, trying to get me to dance with them but I only wanted to dance with your mom." Dad was beaming.

"Al, you are so full of it. I danced. I just didn't want to dance every single dance." I could tell Mom was embarrassed.

Dad said, "You and Uncle Albert don't like to dance, but Aunt Sylvia and I love to dance. Sometimes I wonder if I married the wrong girl." Then he laughed like he was having the time of his life. He knew it always made Mom's face turn red.

"You kids, don't listen to him. He chased me. It didn't matter if I liked to dance or not." Sure enough, her face was red.

Yes, we always had fun at supper when Dad was around.

29. Saving Uncle Albert

Living in Clymer was mostly just fun. We got to go roller skating every Saturday and play with kids in our new neighborhood almost every day. We were really getting good at making new friends no matter where we lived.

One day, Dad came home from work and he was very upset. He came into the house and quietly motioned to Mom to go into their bedroom.

In a hushed voice he said to Mom, "We got word at work that Albert had a terrible accident. He pushed a tree over with his dozer blade and it flipped around, striking him in the head. They think that tree broke his neck. He's in the hospital in Elkins, West Virginia. The doctors don't expect him to live. Please pack me some clothes while I take a bath. I'll leave as soon as possible."

Remember, Uncle Albert was Dad's twin brother. Dad was on the road to Elkins quickly and we were all praying for Uncle Albert to live. Elkins is about a hundred miles from Clymer. Aunt Sylvia, just like Mom, didn't have a driver's license. Our cousins, Maxine, Judy and Larry, were too young to stay at home alone while Aunt Sylvia was at the hospital with Uncle Albert.

Since Dad and Uncle Albert worked for the Meyers Company, Dad knew a lot of the workers who were on the same job as Uncle Albert in Elkins. Dad was sure their families would help Aunt Sylvia with the kids, but he needed to be there to drive her back and forth to the hospital. It was a difficult drive on the way to the hospital, not knowing if he would even be able to say good-bye to his twin brother.

Once he arrived, he hurried down the hall and found Aunt Sylvia standing at the end of the hall, tears running down her cheeks.

She told him, "Al is still alive but he's just lying on a gurney in the hall. They don't give him a chance and they won't do anything for him. I don't know what to do."

Dad sprang into action. "Let me talk to the doctor. They have to do something, at least give him some pain medicine."

He pleaded with the doctor every chance he got; that night, the next morning, the next night, until two whole days had passed. Finally, the doctor did something. He put a screw in Uncle Albert's skull and hung a weight from a chain to put pressure on his neck. Still on a gurney in the hall, he stayed that way for two more days.

By then, Grandma Quinn had arrived on a train and was also begging the doctors to do something. At last they decided he would live and started treating him like a patient instead of an obstacle in the hall. With a brace on his neck, some pain medicine and the love of his family, he was on the mend.

We had no telephone so our news arrived slowly. Every other day or so Dad sent news to the job, and one of the workers who lived close by brought a note to us to keep us up to date. I don't remember how long Dad was gone, but we were really happy when he got home. It took a while before Uncle Albert could go back to work, but when he did, he and Dad decided they would always work on the same job from then on. We were all very thankful for Uncle Albert's miracle.

30. An Unwelcome Visitor

While Dad was in West Virginia visiting Uncle Albert in the hospital, we had a memorable day. It was a summer morning when as usual we kids were running in and out of the house, just to make sure we didn't miss out on anything. Mom was putting bread dough in the tins so it could rise before baking. There was a knock at the door.

Pat opened the door. The lady standing there walked right in, walked over to the table and sat down. Mom didn't recognize her. In fact, she was sure she didn't know her. As Mom looked her over, she felt uneasy. This lady was strange. She had men's shoes on her feet that were way too big. She was wearing a shabby jacket that was ill fitting and out of style. Her uncombed hair was partly covered by a small cap tilted to one side.

"Do you live around here?" Mom asked.

The lady shook her head no.

"Is there something I can do for you?"

Mom looked around to see who was still in the house, hoping it would be Pat.

The lady spoke, "I was just in the neighborhood and hope you can lend me some money. I need to get to Pittsburgh and I'm short on money."

"I'm sorry, I can't lend you money. How are you going to get to Pittsburgh?" Mom asked.

"I'm going to walk. I can walk really fast and it's only a few miles," she said.

Mom then realized something was seriously wrong. Pittsburgh was at least sixty miles west of Clymer, too far for this lady to walk. Then Mom noticed the lady eyeing the hatchet Pat had left on the bench close to the table.

Mom spoke quickly, "Pat, take that hatchet and put it away, please. Your Dad will be unhappy you didn't put it away."

Pat grabbed the hatchet and took it into the pantry across the room.

Then the lady said, "I was going to borrow your hatchet and take it to Pittsburgh with me. I need to protect myself, you know."

By this time, Mom knew it was time for action. "Pat, go next door and ask Ronald to come give this lady a lift. She needs to get on her way, NOW. The rest of you kids go outside and play. Get!"

Pat went outside and hurried over to where Mr. Stack (Ronald) was working in the yard. "Mom needs you to get this strange lady out of our house. She wants a ride to Pittsburgh."

"Take her to Pittsburgh? Does your mom know her?" he asked.

"No, she just showed up and walked right in the house. I think there's something wrong with her and I think she even stole the clothes she's wearing because nothing fits."

Mr. Stack walked over to the porch and opened the door. As soon as he saw her he took her by the hand and led her out the door. He walked her to his car and drove away. We watched until they were out of sight, then we all felt very relieved.

We were all still outside playing when Mr. Stack came home about a half hour later. He said hello as he went in our house to talk to Mom. We followed him like he had a tail.

"I'm sure glad I was home to come get her out of the house for you, Hildegard," Mr. Stack said seriously. "She escaped from the Home for the Mentally Disabled. She beat up a female guard and stole a coat that was hanging by the door. I took her to the police station and they are holding her there. She is one of the violent few that lives at the home. I'm sure glad she didn't get violent here."

We all saw how relieved Mom was and knew we had been blessed for not having a violent incident in the kitchen.

Life settled into what we called normal. Soon Dad came home from being with Uncle Albert in the hospital and he told us it was time to move again. Next stop: Parkersburg, West Virginia.

PARKERSBURG, WEST VIRGINIA
August 1944

31. Parkersburg

When we got to Parkersburg it was still summer, with just a few weeks left before school started. Our most important job was to go meet all the new kids we'd go to school with and learn their favorite games. Pat and I were going to be in seventh grade. Joan was starting fifth grade and John third grade. Romaine was five and Ann was two so they were not in school yet.

We didn't live right in Parkersburg. We lived in the country about ten miles out of town in a house owned by the church just down the road. It was always difficult for Dad to find a house for us because no one wanted to rent to a family with so many kids. The minister told Dad his church loved kids and would be happy to have us.

It was a nice house with a big yard on a not too busy gravel road only about twenty yards from the house. We could have had a garden except it was too late in the year to plant one. It was something to look forward to for next Spring. We had a garden whenever possible because Dad loved farming. In fact, Mom and Dad were buying a farm in Wisconsin to move to when he could afford to quit bulldozing and start farming. The farm was a few miles outside of Rice Lake, across the road from Aunt Rose and Uncle Ralph's farm. It was going to be the perfect place. We would be able to use some of Uncle Ralph's equipment and Dad would help him with his farm work to pay him back.

When we still lived in Markville, Pat and I used to go stay with Aunt Rose and Uncle Ralph for a week or so every summer. We loved it there. I wanted to be a farmer just like Dad did. We'd have cows and a horse to ride, a big garden with all kinds of fresh vegetables. Most of all, we wouldn't be moving all the time. I didn't mind moving but Mom hated it. We never seemed to be all unpacked before we started packing again headed to another new town just down the road.

Because there wasn't too much time before school started, we roamed around the area, meeting new friends and discovering all the different stories about the people and history of the town. The best roamer of the Quinn kids was John. He loved to see how everything was made, what each thing did, and wanted to take everything apart. He and I had more than one fight when he wanted to take my wrist watch apart.

A dirt road ran up the hill on the side of our house. The elementary school was at the top of the hill and it was a true country school. Pat and I were to ride the bus into Parkersburg while the younger kids would attend the school on the hill. John, Joan and Romaine decided to look around to find out who had kids going to the country school. Joan got tired of looking and headed home while the boys kept on checking out the neighborhood.

Close to the school was a dirt road leading away from the school and out of sight. The boys turned down the road until they reached a creek that was only about two feet wide. That interested them so much that they followed the creek upstream to see where it started. They never found the source of the stream but they found a spot where it was wider; wider but very shallow. What a discovery! They looked around and imagined they could have fun playing here. It wasn't long and it was time to go home for supper. All the way home they talked about what they could do to have more fun the next day.

They couldn't wait to head back to play in the little creek. They played there the next day and the next. No one worried about them. They had taken shovels and the wagon with them; the perfect tools to make a dam. Every day for a couple of weeks they worked at finishing the dam so they could go swimming in the pond they had made. The rest of us were all working hard to get settled in our new house and get our stuff put away because school had now started.

Then the weather changed and we had some rainy weather where it wasn't fit to play outside. We played games and were a real nuisance to Mom. After about a week of rainy weather it was time for supper and for Dad to come home. He would be wet and muddy but hungry and supper needed to be on time.

Dad came home and we were about to sit down to supper when someone knocked on the door. Pat answered the door and saw a man standing there.

"Is your dad home? I'd like to talk to him, please," the man said.

"Dad!" Pat yelled. "There's a man here to talk to you."

John leaned over and said to Romaine. "Let's get

out of here. That's the man that drives by and honks his horn when we're working on the dam."

"What does he want to talk to Dad for?" asked Romaine. "Dad doesn't know we built a dam."

"We need to hide. He'll tell Dad I've been skipping school. Dad still doesn't know I got an F on my homework and I can't go back to school until he knows about it," John answered. "That will be the end of us making a dam." John and Romaine disappeared upstairs.

Dad went over to the door and invited the man in. After all the introductions Dad said, "How can I help you?"

"I need to tell you, you have a couple of good boys here," the man said. "They are polite, hard-working and really smart."

Dad sensed something and said, "There's a *but* coming, I can tell. But what?"

"I live down the hill on the other side of the school. Your boys have been playing in the little creek back on my property. They asked if they could and I said it was fine. They brought shovels and a wagon so they could haul dirt and rocks to make a dam. I've seen them there just about every day during school hours and now we have a problem."

"They built a pretty large dam, but the rain washed it out last night. It also washed out part of one of my flower beds but that's not the worst. The water flooded my basement. I have over a foot of water down there and no floor drain for it to escape."

Dad was stunned. It took a few seconds to understand what the boys had done. "You're telling me that my son John has been skipping school, and he's been taking Romaine along as an accomplice?"

"So it seems," the man answered.

"I'll come look at your damage as soon as I talk to the boys," Dad said. The man agreed, thanked Dad and headed home.

"John and Romaine, come here!" Dad yelled through the house. The boys were at Dad's feet in an instant, then they were gone out the door on their way to look over the damage they had caused. Dad lectured them both the whole way.

I'm not sure how they got the water out of the basement or who fixed the flower bed. I do know that John never skipped school again while we lived there. He found more ways to get in trouble, though, which was a way of life for him.

At Dad's jobsite in Parkersburg, WV. August 1944.
Rose Mary (11), Romaine (5), Ann (2) and John (8)
Photo Courtesy Judy Quinn McConnell

32. St. Margaret Mary's

On the first day of school, Pat and I rode the school bus in to Parkersburg. We met all kinds of new kids and they were full of questions.

"Where did you move from?"

"What grades are you in?"

"Will you go to our church?"

"We're in seventh grade. We came from Pennsylvania and we won't go to your church because we're Catholic," Pat answered.

"Catholic? I bet you want to go to the Catholic school. We drive right past it on the way to school," one of the kids said.

I said, "There's a Catholic school? Pat, let's go there!"

Pat just looked at me and shook his head. "Rose Mary, we have never been to a Catholic school. We better ask Mom and Dad if it's okay when we get home from school."

One of the girls looked at me and asked, "Do you

want to go there?" I quickly nodded my head yes. That sounded great to me, but Pat was reluctant.

"Mr. Franks, these kids want to get off at the Catholic school," another girl spoke up.

"Okay, I'll let them off there," replied the bus driver.

The bus stopped and I got off with a couple of other kids. Pat sure wasn't about to get in trouble if he didn't stick with me all day, so he jumped off the bus after us. I read the sign, **St. Margaret Mary's School**. This was going to be special! We had gone to catechism wherever we lived, but this was school. They had nuns to teach us and give us a more complete understanding of our religion. We walked into the school and just stood there, not knowing what to do next.

It only took a minute before a student came by. He smiled at us and said, "I'll tell Sister Katherina that someone's here to see her."

He disappeared into a classroom and we waited. In a minute a nun in her black flowing robe came through the door to meet us. She smiled but had a quizzical look on her face. We waited for her to speak, until she finally said, "What can I do for you?"

Pat and I looked at each other imploring each other to speak. Pat said, "It was your idea for us to come here, you tell Sister why we are here."

I looked at Sister and said, "When we were on the bus some of the kids said if we got off the bus here we could go to this school. So here we are."

Sister broke into a big grin. "Where are your parents? Where do you live and what bus did you take to get here?"

I said, "Mom's at home with our little brother and baby sister. Dad's at work. We live out in the country and a school bus left us off out front. The driver said he'll be back to pick us up at 3:10."

"Well, we'll keep you here until the bus comes to pick you up. In the meantime, come on into my class and I'll introduce you to my students."

We walked into her classroom and she said, "Children, we have two students who would like to come to our school. So, they'll take seats for now and I'll get our day started."

Sister Katherina gave assignments to her students and they began doing their work. She came and sat beside us so we could talk.

"Now, please tell me what grade you're in and where you came from to get here."

I answered, "We're in the seventh grade. Over the summer we moved here from Clymer, Pennsylvania. We didn't go to school there because we only lived there for a couple of months. Our last school was in Moon Run, Pennsylvania. That's where we finished sixth grade. Now we're here and we need to go to school in Parkersburg."

Sister looked apprehensive after hearing this, but continued her questions. "When can your parents come to school to get you enrolled?"

I answered, "I'll ask. We don't have a phone so no one can call. Mom can't drive either."

Sister took a deep breath and said, "Well, I need to talk to an adult before I can enroll you. Have your parents send a note for tomorrow until one of them can come see me. In the meantime, I'll give you some work to do to see if you are ready to be in my class. You can take a letter home with you tonight to explain our school rules."

We nodded our heads and she went back to the front of the room. Pat wasn't happy. "We should be in school somewhere as students, not visitors."

"I think it will be great to go to school here," I said. "I will try to convince Mom and Dad to let us stay here at St. Margaret Mary's."

When it was time to get on the bus after school, Sister said she was glad we came and hoped we'd be able to stay at St. Margaret Mary's for the rest of the school year. She handed Pat a letter to give to Mom and Dad so they could sign it and we could bring it back the next day.

On the bus on our way home, Pat said he wasn't sure he wanted to go to St. Margaret Mary's and asked some of the kids on the bus what it was like in their public school. Most of them said they didn't like it and some said maybe it was okay.

"You be the one to tell Mom and Dad we went to the wrong school all day," Pat lamented. "It wasn't my idea."

"You're just afraid you'll like it and then we'll move again. You hate changing schools and I don't mind at all. They always have something new and different to teach me," I said. "Don't worry, we'll be just fine."

Mom didn't know if she should be happy or sad that we wanted to go to Catholic school. She had that familiar wait and see attitude while we watched the clock until it was time for Dad to come home.

Dad showed up starving, so we decided to wait until after supper was over to spring our surprise. He could tell we had something to say and asked us what was going on as soon as supper was finished.

It was my turn to talk. I had it all planned out in my head what I would say. I'd say, *When we got on the bus this morning one of the kids told us the bus went right by the Catholic school. He also said the driver would be happy to let us off there. When we got inside, Sister Katherine was happy to see us and said we could be students if you'd sign a paper saying it was okay. If you will come to school to meet her and get our school records to her, and, and...*

This is what I blurted out: "Dad, we want to go to St. Margaret Mary's School and we can if you sign a paper that it's okay."

Dad looked at us, looked at Mom, looked at his empty plate, took a deep breath and said, "Okay." He pushed his chair back from the table, got up and walked outside.

Pat and I looked at each other, shrugged our shoulders and cleared the table. Mom just smiled and went about cleaning the kitchen and dining room.

That's how we ended up at St. Margaret Mary's. I loved it there. Each teacher taught two grades. Sister Katherina taught seventh and eighth grade. There were four rooms in the school, with two grades in each room. Seventh and eighth grades were together and we shared the same lessons. Sister Katherina was a wonderful teacher. My favorite subject, math, must have been hers, too. She knew all kinds of shortcuts to get to the right answer in math. She taught us how to do multiplication with three numbers in our heads. I could also divide by three numbers in my head. I never knew anyone who could do that. I felt like a wizard, able to show off my new skill.

I know that school year changed my life. I loved math and learning how to do the problems became a game. We had competitions in school to see who could get to the answer in their head first. We had problems on cardboard test pages with only a small space to write down each answer because all of the figuring was done in our heads. She insisted we all understand everything she was teaching. She found time during the day to sit by any student that was having trouble and encourage them to keep trying. I still do math in my head and I wish more kids today had a teacher like Sister Katherina.

Pat and I were often taken for twins; therefore, Sister Katherina didn't question our being in the same grade. I wasn't about to tell anyone that Pat was older and had been held back in the fifth grade. I enjoyed being in the same grade with Pat.

It was the first time I had been around nuns so the way they dressed in their habits and veils covering their heads seemed strange to me. They didn't mind at all and seemed at ease around everyone, especially Sister Katherina.

33. The Christmas Program

Sister Katherina was truly pleased to be in charge of the Christmas program at St. Margaret Mary's. That year she made up her mind to have the most authentic costumes ever and wanted everyone to feel the reverence the Christmas story deserved. We rehearsed, we searched our homes for things that would make appropriate costumes, and Sister called in all the favors people owed her to get just the right props to finish the set so it would be just right.

It was getting close to program time and Sister still searched for ways to improve the total picture. After we finished practice one day, Sister said, "I think we are almost perfect in our costumes and props, but I do wish there was someplace to get sandals for everyone. I know that with your long costumes they won't be seen so easily but I think you all could feel the complete mood if you were wearing sandals."

Nothing more was said about it and we all went home. When Dad got home from work, Pat was talking to him about something and they went outside to do a project. After a while they came in with what looked like the sole of a shoe, made out of wood. Pat had told Dad that Sister wanted sandals and they thought they could do it. They found some rope and attached it to the wood so it looked just like a sandal.

Pat took the sandal to school the next day to show Sister Katherina. Sister approved and was very pleased that Pat had thought of it. They got out paper and pencil and traced everyone's foot to get their size so Pat could make sandals for everyone. Pat and Dad worked hard and finally two days before the program, everyone that needed them had their own sandals for the show.

We had our last practice and felt the program would be a great success. Sister was smiling from ear to ear, very sure that she had accomplished her finest program. Finally, it was show time at St. Margaret Mary's and the room was filled with parents, siblings, cousins and anyone else who could be dragged to our performance. All of us were in our places on stage. I could see Pat in his shepherd's costume as I stood in my beautiful robe and scarf. We both had small parts but were happy to be a part of the play at our new school. We all whispered our fears and excitement to each other until we heard the words, *Open the Curtain.*

The curtain slowly opened and the audience could see a beautiful scene from the days of the birth of Jesus, with children dressed in authentic costumes down to the beards on the boys' faces and the sandals on our feet. All was silent as the actors began to speak and move about the stage.

"What's that?" I whispered to the girl next to me. "Do you hear that strange noise?" I looked around and saw the boy who was playing Joseph was lifting up his foot. We all quickly became aware that the wooden sandals were very noisy on the wood stage. We hadn't practiced with them on the stage, and didn't realize how noisy they were.

As Mary came on stage it sounded like a pony clip-clopping around us. As more actors moved around, the noise multiplied and you couldn't hear the dialogue. There was a whisper going through the audience, and it became louder with every movement on stage. Then people started to laugh at this strange kind of clicking, tapping sound.

The actors stopped, wondering why everyone in the audience was laughing. You could tell people were trying to conceal their laughter but they just couldn't do it.

Dad was in the back of the room sitting next to Father Summers, the head of the school. Father had brought two other priests with him and all four of them were laughing. They laughed so loud that it was all anyone could hear. The audience turned around to see what Father Summers would do and all action on stage just stopped.

It only took a few moments more to realize the show was over. The crazy sound of the wooden sandals on the hard wood floor was impossible to cover up. If we had been tap dancing it still would have been funny. We couldn't even wiggle our toes without causing the noise. Most of the actors on stage joined in the laughter and then we all went back stage and took off our wooden clip-cloppers.

Sister was heart-broken. Pat never said how he felt. I overheard Dad telling someone it was so funny that Father Summers fell off his chair, but he didn't want Pat to know because he had worked so hard making sandals for everyone.

The biggest topic at school that week was *click, clack, clop, clop*. After a few days, Sister Katherina said, "That will be the last anyone says about our program. We know it was a good program and that is that."

34. A Baby for Christmas

Winter in Parkersburg was snowy and rainy. We did get some sledding in but it only lasted a day or two. We only got an inch or two of snow at a time and we'd wear down the snow to the bare ground pretty quickly. Or, it would warm up and the snow would melt and it was one big muddy mess.

We had been so busy at school practicing for the play that we didn't notice Mom had gained a lot of weight. Boy, did we get a surprise a couple of days after Christmas. We were on school vacation so we could sleep in. On December 27, 1944, I was the first one up and discovered that Mom and Dad were gone in the car.

When Dad drove up, we went to see if they had brought us any more presents. I was surprised to see Dad was alone. I thought, *Where is Mom?* When Dad got out of the car he didn't bring anything with him. In those days, no one told anyone anything about babies, so even though I was in the seventh grade I hadn't heard a word about a new baby on the way.

As Dad entered the house we all asked questions at once, including, "Where's Mom?"

"Guess what, kids? I found a new baby boy in the hospital. I left Mom there to get to know him before we bring him home."

I wasn't totally stupid. Kids talk and I knew where babies came from, but I wasn't smart enough to realize Mom was pregnant. With our moving, the new school, the Christmas play and just plain going to school and homework, I had missed the obvious signs. Now I knew I really was a hick.

We all gathered around so Dad could tell us more. Of course, he was telling a wild story about how he had found this new baby. We each had our own unique story Dad told us about when we were born. I had heard plenty of them by now. Joan, Pat and I looked at each other and smiled. *I guess we all better go along with the story.* Dad loved telling how somehow he had found us all in strange places and brought us home so we would be a family. This was the first time he had found a baby in the hospital. Being a family was Dad's driving force in life. After all, didn't he drag us everywhere he worked so he could be a full time dad?

A few days later Mom came home with our little brother. A new baby was always so much fun. There were so many of us to hold him that he hardly ever got put down. He never cried if he wasn't hungry. Sleeping all night was easy for him because that was the only time we let him sleep. Our new little brother's name was Dennis. He was named after Dad's Grandpa Dennis Quinn, who had lived through the Civil War only to come back to the home farm and end up the victim of an accident.

Grandpa was leading a team of horses pulling a load of wood he was hauling to town. They were on the road approaching a bridge when something spooked the horses. The runaway team surprised Grandpa and he lost control. He grabbed the reins and pulled, causing the wagon to swerve on the bridge. It was a country bridge that had no side rails. Off the bridge went the wagon, the load of wood, the horses and Grandpa, crashing thirty feet below into a river. Grandpa drowned.

I heard Uncle John and Dad talking one time about how they couldn't understand how Grandpa made it through the Civil War, surviving a terrible Confederate Prisoner of War camp in the South, only to be killed by a runaway team of horses in a time of peace.

Before we knew it, Christmas vacation was over and we headed back to school. Life was back to normal – as normal as it can be for a house with seven kids.

35. Pot Belly Stove

February and March brought true winter to us in Parkersburg. It wasn't nearly as cold as it was in Minnesota, but the bitter wind still seemed to go right through us. We had a different source of heat everywhere we lived. In Markville, we had a wood furnace in the basement that heated the whole building. In Moon Run, we had a flat top stove for cooking in which we burned coal. In Crane, we had a fuel oil furnace – what a joy. We didn't need heat in Clymer, because we were only there for the summer.

Parkersburg, West Virginia gave us a pot belly stove. It stood four feet high in the corner of the living room. We used coal and sometimes wood. On cold mornings we gathered around it to warm ourselves before going outside to catch the school bus. I remember the pot belly stove had a big "211" at the top and in large letters in the middle it said, "DEAL OAK."

John, who was in third grade, was always cold and

stood by the stove until the last second before heading to school. Sometimes he even had his coat on while he stood there. One cold March morning Mom was in the kitchen cleaning up after breakfast. She smelled something hot. While she looked around to see where it was coming from the smell changed. Now it smelled like she had left the iron sitting on a shirt on the ironing board. She didn't even have the ironing board up.

When she walked into the living room she was amazed to see a whiff of smoke coming from behind the pot belly stove. She turned the corner to see John standing with his back to the stove and smoke rising off John's back.

"Get away from that stove! You're on fire!" she yelled.

John jumped away from the stove, surprised by the panic in Mom's voice. Mom grabbed him and turned him around. There on the back of his sweatshirt was DEAL OAK backwards. It looked like it had been branded on his sweatshirt.

"You've ruined your sweatshirt! Are you burned anywhere?" she asked, pulling the sweatshirt off over his head.

"Mom, what are you doing? I'm cold," John said, completely unaware of the danger he was in.

"John Quinn, you'll be the death of me yet," Mom said. "I thought the house was on fire! Are you crazy to stand that close to the stove? Go and get a different sweatshirt to wear to school." I could hear the desperation in Mom's voice.

"I didn't feel a thing," John said in a matter of fact way. "I can't help it if I'm so cold all the time."

Mom took the sweatshirt away trying to figure out what to do with it. In the end, since we lived in a small, poor country town, John wore his sweatshirt to school and no one even asked him what happened. I'm sure that wasn't the first time a kid's sweatshirt had been branded by a pot belly stove, and certainly not the last.

36. A Terrible Crash

Dad was the lead bulldozer operator on the site where they were building a new airport outside of Parkersburg. The airport would bring new business to this part of West Virginia. They wanted it completed quickly, so Dad worked long hours. Winter turned to Spring, which meant lots of rain and storms.

One day in April 1945, we came home from school and Dad was already home. I immediately wondered what was wrong. Dad said there had been an accident out at the new airport site. An army airplane had crashed. He paused, clearly filled with grief.

Dad continued, "The storm had passed. It rained hard during the night but the clouds were moving off to the north. The air was fresh and crisp. Off in the distance I could hear the sound of an airplane motor. It sounded low and slow. Suddenly, just above the tree tops I could see a plane. It didn't look like a passenger plane, but more like a private one. As it cleared the trees, it got lower, so low it looked like it wanted to land.

"*It can't land here!* I yelled to the other workers. You see, we have cleared what will someday be a runway, but right now it's a muddy field with grass and brush pushed away by bulldozers." He looked at each one of us kids as he was telling the story.

Dad continued, "We were all afraid of what was about to happen and watched in realization that this plane did want to land. Now, the plane was almost beside us and we saw the door open with two young men in Army uniforms standing there. The engine started sputtering and quit. The plane was out of fuel with no place else to go. It was now apparent that it was going to crash.

"It seemed to be in slow motion, like time was standing still for that horrible last one hundred yards as the plane crashed into the ground. I immediately ran toward the plane. The other men yelled at me to stay away – asking *What if it blows up? What if it catches fire?* and so on.

"I only knew that there were young men in that airplane, young men in the Army who needed help. What if one of them were one of you kids?

"I got to the wrecked plane, found the open door and forced my way in. There were seven of them, seven young men strewn like dolls all broken where they had been thrown by the impact. It was so silent, so ear shatteringly silent that I started to cry. I was sure no one was alive, but I hurried to get them out and away from the plane just in case it did explode.

"I did that heartbreaking job all by myself until finally one of the other men came to take the last man from my arms." Dad hesitated and said slowly, "Not one of those boys lived through the crash."

Dad couldn't tell us any more just then, he was crying so hard. We learned later that the plane was a trainer that had gotten lost in the storm and was way off course. It was 1945 and World War II was raging. Unfortunately, we never did find out who they were or what Army base they were stationed at. Dad wondered if their parents ever heard of how he had tried to save them. Those young men had made an impression on him even though they were only in his life for a few hours. We all learned that any hour can bring a complete change to your life, and not always a happy change.

Right about the time when school was over for the summer, Dad came home and told us we were moving again. We all had reason to regret leaving Parkersburg. We had a nice home, good friends, and Pat and I attended our first Catholic school where learning was both challenging and fun. It felt like home, and we were truly a part of the community.

We packed up and headed off to Reed, West Virginia, a small town with a post office, a store, and a highway that went into Charleston, the state capital.

REED, WEST VIRGINIA
July 1945

37. The House on Stilts

Dad was as old as the hills and Mom was ten. That's what we always told people when they asked about our parents. We had no clue how old hills looked, but we did know that Mom was only a whisper taller than five feet, probably about a hundred pounds and always looked really young. Even when I was in high school people I didn't know would stop me and ask if I was Mom's sister.

Mom and Dad were of the generation when parents never ever argued in the presence of their children, the final decision was always the man's, and like it or not, the wife had no say on how the money was spent. I guess that's why we lived in some of the *Who in their right mind would make their family live there?* places.

When we lived in Minnesota, we were considered to be somewhat well-off, with Dad owning the grocery store and also being post master, train depot agent and selling gasoline to the few locals who owned a car. None of those jobs would support a growing family, but together they provided a living we all enjoyed.

I believe Dad had a purpose in arriving after dark to our new home in Reed. We all, including Mom, were too tired to complain after the trip if we could just stretch out flat and not bounce around anymore on rough country roads.

I think the closest I ever came to hearing my parents argue was when we got up the next morning in our new house. Reed was a small town only five miles out of Charleston, but of course we didn't live in Reed. We lived in the last house at the end of the road outside of Reed.

When we looked out the kitchen window facing the creek we saw that we were above the valley. Then when I walked up to the window to get a better look I could see straight down at least twelve feet. Our house was on stilts! I am still amazed when I think back on some of the homes where we lived, especially this one.

There was a porch on the hill side with a door that went into our living room. The living room would also be our everything room. There were two bedrooms, a kitchen and the everything room. John and Pat ended up sleeping in the everything room. Romaine, at five, had a cot in the room that Joan, Ann and I shared, but he slept in with Pat and John most of the time. Dennis was only about seven months old. His crib was in Mom and Dad's room so it was handy to take care of him during the night.

While I was looking out the window I heard Mom say, "Al, this terrible place will kill one of us. How could you bring us here?"

Dad answered in a quiet voice, "I want you all with me, every day. You know how people won't rent to families, no matter how good the recommendations are. The best part is we will be moving before school starts. They will open a job up just outside Washington, D.C. and we will be there for a year."

He was apologizing and at the same time begging her to live there for a short time. He somehow talked her into it. That was before she knew about driving down the middle of the creek because there was no bridge. She didn't know about the copperhead snakes, either. We were unpacked and settled before Dad had to go to work the next morning.

38. The Buttermilk Battle

Our house on stilts was next to the creek and the railroad tracks were just across the creek. We spent a lot of time walking the rails that summer. We would have contests to see who could walk the furthest without stepping off the rail.

We had an ice box in Markville and one in Clymer, but in all the other places we lived there was no place to buy ice. Reed was the same. That meant it was necessary to shop for food every day so nothing had a chance to spoil. I guess when there are seven kids and two parents, most of the time there's nothing left after supper to put in an icebox.

We lived on the far side of the creek and instead of driving two extra miles to the bridge to cross over it, Dad would drive in the creek for about a quarter mile to get home every day. We always had plenty of food to eat, which meant that Dad stopped at the store every day on his way home. He brought us plenty of food, and Mom was a great cook and always kept us full and healthy. There was always homemade bread, jelly, canned fruit and vegetables and dairy products.

We were as wild as ever exploring the woods and up and down the creek daily. It was summer and I was happy being a kid. I believe the rest of my brothers and sisters were happy too. More and more, we learned to rely on each other for friendship after each move.

Then, one day Dad came home with what he called a wonderful surprise. He had two quarts of buttermilk. Sometime in his past, Dad had developed a passion for buttermilk. He was determined to make buttermilk our passion, too. I had tried buttermilk before and I didn't like it. I didn't even like the way it smelled.

"Gardy, get everyone a glass so we can enjoy this buttermilk together," he said to Mom.

I tried to go to the other room so I could skip the buttermilk. It didn't work. I wasn't two feet from the table when Dad stopped me.

"Get back here young lady. You'll miss out on the new tradition I'm starting: buttermilk for everyone as soon as I get home. It will be nice and cold right out of the icebox in the store." Dad was beaming.

My heart sank. *Buttermilk, every day?* I was a kid who knew what she didn't like and no one was going to change my mind, not even Dad. I tried being in the woods when Dad got home. I tried being busy at buttermilk time. I tried drinking it so slow that Dad would be finished eating and leave the table before I finished. I tried everything and it didn't work. The only thing I didn't dare try was spitting the obnoxious milk out.

I became suspicious that Dad was having a great time watching me come up with some new way to not drink my buttermilk. The buttermilk contest lasted all summer. It was so bad that when Dad drove away to his new job in Maryland I almost cheered. It was like I had won the battle – to me that is.

Dad gave up bringing buttermilk home every day after we moved. He'd had his fun and I learned my lesson; just pretend I liked whatever he brought home so I wouldn't have to go through that again.

39. Flash Flood

After living in our very small house on stilts for a while, Mom told Dad that from now on, she was going to look at the place we were going to live before she agreed to move. We all knew she didn't mean it because she didn't drive and when Dad moved on to his new job, we would be stranded.

We got to do all the things kids love to do in the country and stayed safe. Mom's biggest worry was the snakes. The copperheads lived in the woods and up the mountain behind our house. We were warned that copperheads loved to be in a tree and drop down onto anyone walking below. I never saw such a thing, but it kept us all looking up when we were in the woods, and we didn't stray far from home.

It is true, though, that we saw some kind of snake every day. We also saw lizards. The lizards were around five or six inches long and were a beautiful shade of green. They were everywhere, including on our porch. They were so fast we could never catch one. We had to be very careful not to open the screen door if a lizard was near. Mom was sure they were poisonous (they weren't) and she hated them.

Near the end of summer, Dad moved on to his new job in Maryland and we were looking forward to having him come back and move us, just like always in this new way of life. Around the time Dad left, I took the bus to Moon Run to visit with our friends the Mahoney's. Pat had found a summer job in Charleston as a pin setter at a bowling alley. In those days, there were no machines to reset the pins after each round of bowling, so pin setters like Pat would pick up all the pins that were knocked down and reset them by hand to be ready for the next bowler.

On the day I was to return home from Moon Run, it rained hard all day and everyone was stuck in the house. My bus was arriving at 11 PM and Pat was to pick me up at the bus station after his shift at the bowling alley. Pat was there waiting for me right on time and I was happy to see him. Our trip home wasn't going to be easy. The first leg we walked to a bus stop where the bus route was on the far side of the Big Kanawha River because there was no bus on our side of the river that late at night.

Our next mode of transportation was to hitch a ride in a row boat to get across the river. It couldn't have cost much because Pat took this trip every night that he worked. Pin setters made next to nothing and if no one was bowling they were sent home early with empty pockets.

Pat and I got off the bus and went down to the river's edge hoping to be taken across by one of the men who made a living rowing back and forth across the river. We talked to the man who was there with his boat, but he didn't want to give us a ride because it was sprinkling. Pat reminded him that he took this trip almost every night, and the rower finally agreed.

We got a little wet as it started to rain harder, but were grateful that it was warm out even though it was midnight by now. Once we got across the river we had a long walk through a field to get to the creek by our house. We finally made it to the creek and were both shocked to see how high the water was. Instead of being knee deep, the water was close to waist deep. Now we both had to wade through the creek.

I had a suitcase and a paper shopping bag. Both were filled with gifts from our friends and things I had bought in Pittsburgh. Now Pat was upset.

"We need to leave this stuff here for the night. It will get wet trying to cross the creek when it's this high," he said.

"We can't leave it here; it's raining," I pleaded. "I have some really good stuff in here. Everyone at Mahoney's house sent something back with me. Please, we have to take it all."

"Junk. You're always dragging junk around for everyone," Pat said, frustrated.

"You can call it junk but I have a present for you, too."

Pat gave in. "Well, I guess if you can carry the bag, I can get your suitcase across for you."

Pat looked up, wondering if he could get the suitcase across on the cables he walked across nightly. At one time there had been a walking bridge here. Since it hardly got used, the local people had let it fall apart and all that remained was the cables that used to hold boards for walking across. Pat climbed up and started across.

"I can make it. You get started across," I said.

I took my shoes off, put them in the bag and stepped into the creek. Instantly, I realized the water was much deeper than I expected. It was so strange. The water was deep but there was little current. Another step and it was up to my arm pits. It was just like someone had dammed up the creek. Now I was really scared. A couple of more steps into the water and I felt the current getting strong, which surprised me. I knew I was in trouble with that shopping bag, trying to hold it over my head. A couple of more steps and a package fell out of the top of the bag. Just like that it was floating downstream. Would I be able to get all the way across without losing everything? Just last week when I crossed here, the water was only half way to my knees.

Pat was calling out, telling me to hurry. I knew I needed to hurry, but the water was taking my feet from where I tried to put them down. The current was starting to carry me away and I started crying. I knew I couldn't make it. My mind immediately flashed back to the time Pat and I almost drowned in the icy waters of the Tamarack River in Minnesota and I started to panic. I cried out for Pat to help me.

Pat had made it across by then. He set the suitcase down, jumped in the creek and started wading toward me. He shouted at me to grab his hand but it seemed like forever before I was finally able to grab his hand and hold on. Another package fell out of the bag. I was so insistent on holding onto that bag even at the risk of my life – it was foolish. With Pat's help we both made it to shore even as the water continued to rise. Never in my life was I more thankful that Pat was there to save me.

The light rain turned into a downpour. We followed the path up the hill to where our house stood. It was a slippery muddy mess and was almost impossible to climb up the hill. I managed to fall down and stop to pick up my precious presents a couple of times. We made it to the house and a few moments later we heard a loud noise like nothing I had heard before. It sounded like a freight train was coming at our house. We ran to the kitchen window and saw a wall of water crushing everything in its path. I realized immediately it was a flash flood.

We ran outside to see the water rushing up the hill toward our house. It was a wall of water bigger than anything I had ever seen. The water came all the way up under our house and started to cover the stilts under our house. That's when Mom grabbed us both, and rushed into the house. Mom yelled, waking all the other kids. She grabbed Dennis out of his crib and the other kids ran out the door with us.

We stayed outside in the rain on the high side of the hill until the wall of water had passed. I don't remember exactly how long we stayed out there, but it must have been several hours. Mom held us all close, thankful that Pat and I had narrowly escaped the flash flood. What if we were in the creek moments later? We didn't even want to think about what might have happened.

Finally, Mom and Pat walked around the corner of the house to see that the water had gone down several feet and was no longer under the house. They inspected the stilts and were happy to see they hadn't moved one bit. Mom suspected the water had been this high before. After a little soul searching, Mom decided we could go back inside for the night. It was too much for her to think of the future at this moment.

Mom started packing the next day. With no phone and no car, there was no way to let Dad know how tragedy had nearly torn our family apart. Somehow she got word to Dad and when he came home in a few days we were ready to move. Fortunately, Dad had found a house and was ready to take us back with him. We were moving to Bowie, Maryland, and we hoped our new house would not be anywhere near a creek.

BOWIE, MARYLAND
August 1945

40. Life Lessons in Bowie

We all packed into the old Plymouth and followed the moving truck all the way to Bowie. When we got to Bowie we could see that the road was paved and wide. Trees lined the road. All kinds of flowers were in bloom in just about every color. The houses were huge with beautiful, large porches, once called verandas, and every house had a chimney. I even saw some houses with two chimneys. I couldn't imagine how rich you would have to be to have two fireplaces. I had never even known anyone with one fireplace.

We were used to cook stoves that burned wood or coal, a furnace or potbelly stove, but fireplaces were for rich people to sit and watch the fire for pure enjoyment. They would have a man servant to clean out the ashes.

As we continued down the road, I thought people in Maryland just had to be different than anyone I had met. They had to be so, so smart! I started dreaming about living in one of these big, beautiful houses. Then we turned off the highway and headed down a narrow dirt road. We drove by a few houses until we arrived at the last house at the end of the road. It was a tiny house. Why would I ever think that we'd live anywhere except in the house at the end of the road? It was smaller than any place we had lived before and we had added another kid to the family.

There were only two windows on the front side of the house, but there were nice shade trees all around the house. It was hot in Maryland, even hotter than in West Virginia. Every time we moved it amazed me that we could somehow pack up everything, jump in a vehicle and land in what seemed like another world in the same day. Markville, Minnesota seemed like a lifetime ago and it had been less than three years.

We had looked at a map and saw that the highway near Bowie went from Baltimore to Washington, D.C. Bowie was closer to D.C. but easily within an hour's drive to either city. I was looking forward to sightseeing in Washington, D.C.

It didn't take long to get the truck unloaded and squeeze all our things into our new tiny house. Since it was August, school was on our minds. We found out all of us school-age kids would ride the bus to Bowie together, then Pat and I would change buses and ride together to our school in Laurel.

The neighbor kids told us this would be the first year that Prince George's County would have eighth grade. Who ever heard of going from seventh grade straight into ninth grade? We were sure they must be lying. Kids had tried telling us crazy stuff when we changed schools before. I knew I would be in eighth grade no matter what they said.

When Dad came home for supper that night he told

us, "Sure enough, kids, it's true. Any student who attended seventh grade last year has the choice to either attend eighth or ninth grade this year. The law used to be that if you finished seventh grade you could quit school, but that law is changing now. This is to be a transition year; next year all seventh graders will go directly into eighth grade. Pat, you and Rose Mary will both be in eighth grade this year"

I was worried that Pat would have to fight the bullies again. Every time we moved Pat had to prove he could win a fight. I guess that's the way it was for kids back then. We would surely find out the first day of school.

We went exploring outside and discovered we did live by a creek, but thankfully it was only about two feet wide. No danger there. Right across the creek was a small one-room schoolhouse. We peeked in the windows and saw a very clean and neat school room. There were pictures on the bulletin board made by students and flowers on the windowsills. Everything was so neat and clean I knew I would enjoy this school. When we talked about it with the neighbor kids they said we couldn't go to school there because it was only for black kids. I thought, *How lucky those kids are to have such a wonderful teacher.*

I was shocked when I found out that schools were still segregated in Maryland. We saw the black kids walking by the house every day on their way to school because they used the path in front of our house to get to school. I said hello and told them I was their new neighbor but they were shy and seemed afraid to talk to me. They just kept walking and didn't say anything. This was my first experience with segregation and it truly bothered me. I was used to talking to everyone and making all kinds of new friends.

We were Catholic and went to mass every Sunday. There was a Catholic church in Bowie about a mile away. Dad had to work our first Sunday in Bowie so Mom stayed home with the little kids, and Pat, Joan and I walked to church. We headed out early and the mile walk was easy for us. We got to church in plenty of time and walked right in like we always did. We headed down the aisle and went all the way to the front of the church and sat down. We kids always sat up front either by ourselves or with Dad. Mom would sit in the back with the baby and littlest kids in case they were noisy. We had to sit up front so Father could correct us if we misbehaved. If Father had to correct us, we would be in big trouble with Dad when we got home. Being so well-trained in how to act in church, we did not turn around when we heard the rest of the congregation being seated. No one sat in the front row with us.

Joan whispered to me, "These people are noisy. If we did that Dad would make us sit on a chair when we got home."

I said, "Well, maybe they have stuff to talk about before Father comes out to the altar."

Then Pat poked me in the ribs and said, "Don't look now but we are the only white people here. No wonder they're whispering."

I sneaked a peek and sure enough we were seated among all black people. Then Father came out of the sacristy to start mass. When people came up to receive communion I saw there were white people in line along with black people.

When mass was over we weren't sure what we should do. We looked behind us to see the church had filled for mass but all the white people were in the back. The black people around us didn't leave until the back of the church had emptied. We waited and walked out with them. As we left the church a man came over to tell us about the "custom" of seating at that church.

Since moving to Maryland we learned the schools were still segregated and now everyone could go to the same church but certain seats were for certain races. It sure seemed dumb to me. Then we found out that all the other churches around were completely segregated, either black or white. We had a big discussion about it with Mom and Dad later that day.

Dad said firmly, "It might be the tradition here in Maryland but we are going to do as we always have. We will not see any difference in people no matter what color or race they are. When you meet someone new, pretend you are blind. Listen to how they say things more than what they say. In other words, look for their intent and their heart. Then you can judge their character." That is how I've tried to see people my whole life.

From then on we sat in the middle of the church, somewhere between the black people in the front and the white people in the back. This certainly was a new life for us, and I figured out very quickly that I didn't like segregation.

41. John's Dress

We'd lived in cabins, coal towns, on the other side of the creek and now out on a tobacco farm in Maryland. Maryland is as different from Minnesota as winter is from summer. Tobacco and cotton, peaches and pears, magnolias and rhododendrons were growing here; so many plants I had never seen before.

There were plantations, sailboats out in Chesapeake Bay and the tide was going out and coming in. It was like a dream world filled with so many wonderful things. Downtown Washington, D.C. was like jumping right into a history book.

However, one dark cloud hung over us. We were all very aware that World War II was still going on. Since we lived between Annapolis, Maryland and Washington, D.C., we were right in the middle of all the war news. Wherever we looked sailors were travelling. It sounded like the war would soon be over, but there were still reports of casualties on both fronts. Uncle

John and Uncle Francis were still serving in the war in the Pacific and we were worried they might be hurt before it ended.

Once we started school, we had to walk about a quarter mile out to the main road to catch the school bus. John was now in the fourth grade. He found all kinds of ways to delay getting to the bus. One day he was being the biggest slowpoke I have ever seen. I was in charge of seeing to it that John got on the bus, but I just couldn't get him going and we missed the bus. We walked back home and John thought it was a wonderful day. Mom had given up on trying to keep John in line, so he had a great time all day – until Dad got home from work. Dad was very upset when he found out I had missed a day of school because of John.

John, Dad and I had a meeting. Dad did all the talking. "John, you are acting like a spoiled little girl; therefore, you will have to dress like a girl." Mom got one of Joan's dresses out of the closet and put it on a chair.

The next morning Dad waited to see to it that John wore that dress. We headed for the bus stop and Dad left for work. The one thing about Dad; he always had time to make sure we kids did what was expected of us.

John stood at the back of the line as we waited for the bus. He knew Dad would take him to school if he didn't get on the bus, so he got on with the rest of us when the bus came. The other kids on the bus noticed him wearing a dress but they didn't say much. John glared at them as if to say, *Go ahead, say something. I dare you!* John's reputation of fighting probably helped him in this situation.

When we got to school, John wouldn't get off the bus. I had to go or I would miss my bus to school in

Laurel. When I stepped off the bus, there was Dad, big as life, waiting with John's regular clothes in hand. I gave Dad a hug and ran to my bus. As we were pulling out of the schoolyard, I saw Dad and John get off the bus. John was wearing his regular clothes and a big smile. I thought Dad was the smartest man in the whole world.

Nothing was ever said about that morning when we got home, but Dad's genius made my life so much easier. From then on, John was always the first one on the bus, as long as I can remember, no matter where we lived.

42. Visiting Dad at Work

One Saturday morning, not long after we moved to Bowie, John and Romaine decided to go find Dad at work. He was working on a new highway between Baltimore and D.C. It was essential to have another way to evacuate Washington in case of an emergency. Romaine had just turned six, and John was eight. They didn't exactly know where Dad was working on the road, but thought it couldn't be too far from home. They figured they were smart enough to find Dad and started walking.

They didn't even think to bring water, food or money with them, and consequently they got hungry and thirsty. They saw a filling station so they stopped and asked for a drink of water. They began walking along, and pretty soon a man driving by stopped and asked them who they were and where they were going. They asked the man if he knew where the road construction was, because they were going to visit Dad at work. The man asked if Dad knew they were coming, and they told him they were going to surprise him. They hoped they were close, because they were hot, hungry and thirsty. The man kindly pointed down the road and told them to head that way.

The man drove away and headed down the road in the direction John and Romaine were walking. Romaine started to get worried because they were a long way from home and they didn't know where they were. He thought John must be getting worried, too. Now they stopped and stood by the road deciding if they should turn back. Romaine asked, "What should we do now, John? I'm tired, I'm thirsty and I'm scared."

The man in the car decided to drive to the road construction site a little farther down the highway to see if he could find out who the boys were looking for. He got out of his car and walked up to several workers. "Does anyone here have two boys?" he asked. "One's a blonde and the littler one has very dark hair."

One of the workers said, "I don't, but go over by that bulldozer and ask the operator. He may be their dad."

The man walked over to the bulldozer and they talked for a bit, shook hands, and then both men walked over to their cars.

Meanwhile, the boys had decided to turn back. They were walking along the highway hoping they could make it home before supper. Then they heard a car slowly approaching behind them.

John said in his bravest voice, "Don't look back, Romaine. We know where we are and don't tell whoever it is you're hungry, you crybaby."

Romaine was almost crying as he said, "I am so hungry I could eat a horse. I'm too tired to walk anymore and I want a ride. I'm not a crybaby! You're scared, too!"

"I'm not scared! I'll never bring you along on my next adventure. If Joan had come, we'd be there by now. We never would've turned back. She never gets scared like you do."

The car stayed behind them until they couldn't stand it any longer. Romaine turned around slowly and then started yelling, "It's Dad! It's Dad!" I don't think those two boys had ever been so happy to see Dad than at that moment.

They ran over to the car and climbed in the back seat. Dad put the old car in gear and headed home. Dad was singing and acting like they weren't even there the whole ride home. He just let them wait and think about what he would do to punish them. I've had that treatment, and it's far worse than the final punishment.

When they got home, Dad told Mom the whole story. The boys got their punishment and learned a valuable lesson. It wasn't a good time to be two runaway kids. Romaine told me, "That's the last time I will ever go on an expedition with John. He can think up the darnedest things to do and always knows how to get me in trouble." I agreed.

43. The Old '36 Plymouth

It was still wartime when we moved to Bowie. Even though the war in Europe had ended in May, the Japanese did not surrender until September 2, 1945. It was difficult to buy new products because many things were rationed and other things, like new cars, were not being made. Everyone was making airplanes, tanks or Jeeps. Gasoline was one of the things that was rationed; therefore, you needed a ration stamp to buy it. Dad said that even with a ration stamp, service stations would only sell ten gallons at a time, or even less.

Because Dad was on the crew building that vital highway between Washington, D.C. and Baltimore, he received extra ration stamps to travel back and forth to work. Even though he wanted to, Dad couldn't upgrade his car because there just weren't any to buy. Our old 1936 Plymouth had seen better days. It couldn't keep up with the traffic around D.C., but it still got us where we needed to go. It did have a problem that drove Dad crazy: when the temperature dropped, she wouldn't start. Once she started, though, she never failed.

Maryland is not known for very cold weather, but we had a cold spell that fall and it even snowed. The old '36 pulled her *I'm not going to start today* trick and Dad was desperate. He was not a man known to give up over such a thing and he racked his brain for a solution.

Then Dad remembered that he had a small one-burner white gas stove – the kind you have to pump air into the tank to build pressure in order to light the burner. Not knowing what else to do, he decided to try it. He took the stove out into the yard, pumped up the tank and lit the burner. Of course, all of us kids were watching because everything Dad did was interesting to us. Once he had the burner lit he made all of us back up, then he pushed the little stove under the car right beneath the oil pan. After a couple of minutes, he reached under the car, grabbed the stove and turned it off.

"Now let's see if I've heated the oil pan enough to get the old girl to start!" Dad said with a big smile. Dad liked to entertain us whenever he could. He took a deep breath and pushed the starter button. Sure enough, she started. Dad laughed out loud and said, "See, kids? I knew it would work!"

From then on, the little gas stove was put to use whenever the temperature dropped a little, even if he hadn't tried starting her. It got to be such a regular thing that Dad taught Pat how to do it. We thought it was great. Now, whenever it was time to go somewhere, we were able to go.

It wasn't until we moved to Pennsylvania a year

later that we all found out how dangerous it was to put an open flame so close to a gas tank. One winter morning Pat went out and put the lit stove under the car right beneath the oil tank like Dad had taught him. One of the neighbor men came running over, shouting, "What on earth are you doing? You're going to kill yourself!"

Pat looked at him and said, "What do you mean? We do this all the time and nothing has happened!"

The man answered, "You're going to do it one too many times and it'll be the last thing you ever do because it will blow you to smithereens if that old car catches fire!"

By this time, Dad and a bunch of us kids were outside to see what the commotion was all about. The man looked at Dad shaking his head and explained the danger to him. I don't remember Dad ever thinking anything he did was dangerous.

I've never stopped marveling at the fact that we didn't all blow up. That old car leaked oil, had a terrible exhaust problem and who knows what else was wrong with it. But, Dad always found a way to make things work when they were broken.

He always told us, "Kids, if you need something fixed, you've got to find a way yourselves. You may wait forever for someone else to come along and fix it for you, and who has that kind of time?"

All of us kids learned the lesson to figure things out for ourselves because there might not be time to wait for someone to come along and help. I've been told most of my life, "You should have been born a hundred years ago, Rose Mary. You know how to do everything." I was proud to be told I could take care of any problems that came up. Somehow I've managed not to blow anything up or cause any great damage. I guess

God takes care of fools and children. I've certainly been both.

44. Visiting the Doctor in D.C.

When winter arrived in Bowie I got sick again. Back in Markville, I spent almost all of the third grade in bed. When we moved to the eastern states I spent time every winter being sick. Finally, Dad decided it was time for me to get better once and for all.

We started by going to a doctor in Washington, D.C. The doctor said I would need to see him twice a week to have a treatment to clear my sinuses. These trips to the doctor turned into sightseeing tours of D.C. Every time we went Dad took the time to visit a historic site.

Dad loved sightseeing, so the whole family would go on Sundays when he wasn't working. Washington was such a wonderful place just to drive around. Of course, you have to be willing to get lost – a lot. The city is full of circles. Dad would see a building he wanted to visit and would start driving toward it, but either we couldn't get out of the circle where he wanted to exit or we'd go under the street where we wanted to be. We'd end up in a completely different area. We never got to see as much as Dad wanted to see before it was time to go home.

One Sunday we visited the Smithsonian and we heard a lot of people talking about seeing the Hope Diamond. We stood in line a long time to finally see it, but I wasn't impressed. What does a thirteen-year-old country girl know about diamonds anyway?

While Mom and Dad were looking at all the other diamonds I wandered around the room. I was the only one who ended up by a row of cases filled with turquoise. Now that was worth seeing! I looked at case after case of turquoise, admiring hundreds of different shades of blue and green. I immediately fell in love with turquoise. Oh, what a memory!

One time during one of my trips to the doctor, Dad and I went to the U.S. Capitol. It was a rainy day so there weren't very many sightseers there. Dad started talking to one of the guards who told us the painting on the ceiling was being cleaned that day. Dad was interested in the stairway to the capitol dome. The stairway was closed and off limits. After some more conversation with the guard, we discovered that the stairway was closed because of the painting being cleaned.

A little of Dad's Irish charm and we were on our way up the stairs. It was lunchtime for the cleaning crew and if we hurried, we'd be back down before they returned to work. We reached the landing and went out the door to where you can walk around the highest part of the dome. What a thrill! It was like seeing Washington from an airplane. What a beautifully laid out city. I don't know if this area is ever open to the public now, but I remember that view like it was yesterday. The rain had stopped and all the buildings looked clean, shiny and new in the bright sunlight.

On another trip to the doctor, Dad and I went back to the Smithsonian and spent the rest of the day there. What a treasure trove of interesting things. I was impressed by the collection of president's wives' gowns worn for the inaugural ball. Mary Lincoln's gown was my favorite.

The Spirit of St. Louis was hanging in one of the rooms. I stood under it for a long time wondering how Charles Lindbergh managed to stay awake to fly all the way across the Atlantic Ocean and on to Paris. It might seem like nothing now, but in 1927 it was an unbelievable feat.

We saw the Lord's Prayer carved on the head of a pin, machines, jewelry, and all kinds of inventions. The thing that impressed me most that day was the actual American flag that flew over Fort McHenry the night the British shelled it while Francis Scott Key, standing on the deck of a British ship holding American prisoners, wrote the Star Spangled Banner.

I couldn't believe how big the flag was. Originally it was 34 by 42 feet. Through the years, relics had been cut from it and now it was 34 x 34 feet. One of the stars had been removed. There were other holes, which I was sure were from British shells. The flag covered the whole wall all the way down the stairway. What could be more patriotic than this flag? Here it was, a couple of months after the end of World War II, and the inspiration for the Star Spangled Banner was right there in front of me. I still feel a surge of pride in my chest when I remember how I felt that day.

Dad and I went to the Smithsonian several times while I was going to the doctor so often. Dad found time to visit so many places, it was almost a pleasure being sick. In the end, when my sinus problem was cleared up, I went in and had my tonsils and adenoids removed. I improved so much that after the surgery I was generally in great health at last.

Here I am, age 13, enjoying myself and feeling much better! Bowie, MD 1946

45. Jack Armstrong Contest

When Spring came it was cherry blossom time in Washington, D.C. The whole countryside was filled with colorful flowers and bushes. I don't know if I had ever seen anything so beautiful.

Jimmy, one of our neighbors, came over to ask if any of us kids would like to make some money. Of course we said we would. We asked him what we needed to do, and when we found out we were all surprised.

Jimmy said, "I have a field ready for planting and I'm looking to fill it with tobacco."

"Tobacco?" I asked. "What do we know about tobacco?"

"It's just like planting cabbage plants," Jimmy said. "Be very careful not to break the fragile stock and make sure you get the dirt around it so the roots won't get air."

Pat and I asked Dad if it was okay and he agreed, saying it would be hard work. It was a learning experience for me. I had helped plant cabbage before, but only about twenty-five plants. Now we were planting a five-acre field. Jimmy's son helped and there were one or two other kids, but it was still a lot of work for us. I don't know how many plants we put in the ground, but I was sick of it by the time we finished. We each got paid twenty-five cents a day and we thought it was great.

Jimmy said we did a great job so we must not have broken too many plants. I had never seen a tobacco field before and as the plants grew through the spring and summer, I thought the giant leaves were pretty. That was how our summer started and then things got really interesting.

I faithfully listened to a radio program called *Jack Armstrong, the All-American Boy*. The show lasted fifteen minutes and featured Jack Armstrong and his adventures around the world. I always wanted to eat Wheaties for breakfast because Jack ate them every day. I didn't care if he was a boy; I loved adventure, too! After all, Wheaties were the breakfast of champions.

That summer they announced a contest during the radio show. If I won, I would be the proud owner of a Piper Cub airplane. Of course I wanted to enter - who wouldn't want to own a Piper Cub? All I had to do was come up with the winning name for a Piper Cub trainer airplane. I thought about it for a couple of days. I wrote down dozens of ideas, then picked *American Rose*. My heart was filled with hope when I got my Wheaties box top, put it in an envelope with my entry and sent it off in the mail to General Mills in Minnesota.

A few weeks went by and then one day I got a letter in the mail from the Jack Armstrong program. I was so excited – I was afraid to open it! Could I have won the Piper Cub? My heart was pounding as I opened the letter. Well, I didn't win the plane, but I did win second prize in the naming contest. I was to get a ride in a Piper Cub along with some flight instructions. I was to wait for another letter that would notify me when and where I'd get my prize.

It seemed like I waited forever before I got another letter from the Jack Armstrong program. I was really disappointed when I read that I would not get to fly in a Piper Cub after all. Instead, my prize was a commercial flight for one from Washington International to Philadelphia and back again two hours later. I was so disappointed not to have my flight in a Piper Cub that I had tears in my eyes. I had been dreaming of sitting next to the pilot so he could show me how to fly the plane.

My flight was scheduled for a Sunday afternoon a couple of weeks later. Here I was, thirteen years old, and I was flying to Philadelphia by myself. Mom and Dad didn't seem worried at all when they took me to the airport. They waved as we taxied to the runway. Off I went into the wide blue yonder. This was my very first flight. I was the first person in my family to fly. What bragging rights! I was too young and clueless to be scared. I was just a kid with lots of questions and no pilot to answer them.

The stewardesses were too busy to have any time for me on such a short flight. It was a one-hour flight to Philadelphia, a two-hour layover and then one hour back to D.C. The Philadelphia airport was out in the country so all I could see were trees and fields. I had no time or money to go see any sights. I just sat in the airport waiting for them to tell me to board for my return flight.

One of the ticket clerks thought I was stranded because no one came to pick me up. He wanted to call the police to come get me. I had to convince him that I didn't need the police. Once he had a look at my return ticket he finally believed that I wasn't abandoned.

"It's a pretty mean trick for them to send you on this trip all by yourself. They just dropped you off with no one here or anything for you to do but get in trouble." He walked over to the pop machine and bought me a Coke.

By the time I drank my Coke it was time for my return flight. All went well and before I knew it I was back in D.C. Mom and Dad were there waiting to hear all about my wonderful trip.

I said glumly, "It was boring. I didn't get to see anything. I was the first one of us to fly, so I guess that's something to tell everybody."

I have to admit, they all acted like it was no big deal with me being the first to fly in an airplane. Maybe I did brag a little more than I should have, but I didn't get to brag very often.

46. Camping Out

That summer John was nine and Romaine was six. They were always looking for fun things to do. On a warm Saturday, John rode the bike up and down the driveway for a while. There wasn't anyone around to show off in front of so it took some of the fun out of it. He thought, *Now what? I should look for Romaine so we can do something together.*

He went around the back of the house and found Romaine playing with our Labrador Retriever, Susie. Romaine was throwing a stick for Susie to chase, which didn't look too exciting to John.

"Hey, Smokey Joe, want to have some fun?" Smokey Joe was the nickname Romaine had been given because someone told Dad he was smoking Indian tobacco, a weed that had little seeds hanging off a branch and turned brown when it got ripe.

Romaine shook his head, saying, "This is fun. Susie brings the stick back to me every time!"

"I mean real fun like going camping," John said.

Romaine's eyes lit up. "Going camping? Did Dad say he'd take us camping?"

"I don't mean with Dad. I mean you, me and Susie. Maybe Fennel can come too." Dave Fennel was one of John's friends that lived just down the road. Everybody called him by his last name.

"How can we go camping if Dad doesn't take us?" Romaine asked.

"We can pack up our stuff on the bike. I know a place by the creek where we can camp and go fishing. Sounds like lots of fun, right?" John was trying hard to convince Romaine to go along.

"What will we eat?" Romaine asked. "Mom's not here and we'd have to make our own stuff."

John answered, "That's not too hard. We can go see what's in the kitchen. Mom won't care."

Getting up, Romaine said, "Come on, Susie. Let's go."

John parked the bike and they went in the house to get ready for the camping trip. It took a while but they finally got everything packed on the bike. It was too full to ride, so they pushed the bike. They walked to Fennel's house to see if he could come along, but his mom wasn't home either. They hung around for a while waiting for Fennel's mom to come home.

They ran out of patience and decided to head to the creek. "I'll meet you at the creek if I'm allowed to come," Fennel said.

As they walked up the road they saw a car coming. It was Dad. He stopped to ask where they were going. "What are you two up to? You look like you're headed for open spaces."

Romaine answered proudly, "We're going camping."

"Going camping? Where?" Dad asked.

"Right over by the creek. See that tree? We'll be

right there," John said.

Dad smiled, "Looks like a good place. Do you have enough food? How about blankets for the night?"

John stuck out his chest and put his shoulders back. "We have all that stuff. We can even go fishing."

"I see Susie is with you," Dad said. "Don't let her follow me home. You'll need her."

Dad drove away, just beaming thinking about the two boys. He figured they would come home as soon as it started to get dark. Mom was home when Dad got there.

As he walked in the house he said, "Hi there, girl. Where is everybody? There's not a kid outside to say hello."

Mom gave him a kiss and answered, "I've only been here a few minutes. No one was here to greet me either. Ann and Dennis are sleeping. What do you know about the rest of the kids?"

"I saw John and Romaine down the road past Fennel's house on their way to go camping for the night, down by the creek."

Mom was agitated. "Who said they could go camping? That's no place for two little kids to spend the night. How could you let them?"

Dad said calmly, "They have food, blankets and Susie. You know Susie will never let anything happen to those boys. As soon as it gets dark they'll head home. Scared to death."

"I'll be scared to death first," Mom said. "We should send Pat to tell them to come home."

"Gardy, when Pat was nine back in Markville, he and Robert camped out all the time. You never said a word," Dad replied.

"Right," Mom said. "They were camped in the yard with a fence around it. You can't possibly think this is the same. Please send Pat to go get them."

"Let's at least let them have their supper first," Dad said. "They will be back as soon as they run out of food. Romaine is always hungry at bedtime. They aren't babies any more," he reminded her.

A while later, back at their campsite, Romaine said, "John, let's eat. I'm hungry."

"We've already eaten all the stuff we brought for supper. Are you going to eat your breakfast now?" John asked.

"No, but what else can I eat? I can't have any fun when I'm hungry," Romaine said.

"We haven't been fishing yet. I want to catch a fish, don't you?" John said.

Romaine nodded and they started fishing. The boys had no idea the only thing you could catch in this creek were frogs and tadpoles. At least it kept Romaine's mind off of food.

After we finished supper at home, Dad and Pat snuck up close to the boys' campsite to see how they were doing. Everything looked peaceful. Susie was lying next to Romaine and John was holding his fishing pole expecting a fish anytime.

Just then John said, "Boy, it seems like we've been fishing a long time. Well, I guess if you don't catch a fish you don't have to clean it. It sure is fun hoping for a fish though."

Dad smiled, then whispered, "What do you think, Pat? Should we tell them to come home?"

"No, I'd want to stay if I was them. It doesn't look like they're scared," Pat answered.

"We may as well go home. If they don't come home by bedtime, I'll check back to see how they're doing. Come on, Pat, we're not getting much done here. I'll come back later."

Dad and Pat went back to the house to face Mom. She wasn't happy but Dad promised he'd go get the kids before they went to bed. Mom was uneasy about the situation, but she waited it out.

When it was just about dark, Mom and Dad both went to check on the boys at their campsite. Mom was surprised to see that Romaine was sleeping with Susie and John was lying there just looking up at the stars.

"Would you look at that," Dad said. "Those two kids are fine! All of your worrying was for nothing. Here comes Susie – she wants you to know she's on guard. Don't you think we should let the boys stay?"

Mom was reluctant, but despite herself she said, "I guess they're okay, but they're so young. I worry about them."

Dad replied softly, "I remember how hard it was for you to let Pat grow up. Remember? Nothing bad happened then."

"You're right. It's just hard to see them grow up so fast. I guess they're safe with Susie here," Mom said.

"Come on. The boys aren't any further from the house than Pat and Robert were in Markville," Dad said. "We want our kids to be as independent as they were back in Minnesota. This is the first step."

The boys camped out all night and they never knew how many visits Dad made to check on them through the night. It was a good learning experience for all; be brave, but be safe.

47. Mom's Not Home

Even though we had all grown a lot since we left Markville, Joan hadn't changed a bit. You would think by the time she reached the sixth grade she would have grown out of fighting at the drop of a hat. Back in Markville, Joan and two boys in her class were always at odds. It was a regular occurrence for them to come to blows. She always won, mostly because if they got in a punch or two she got madder than a hornet and never stopped swinging until they ran away.

Here in Bowie, one of Joan's new friends in her class was Tommy. She and Tommy liked to hang out regularly. One time they got into a fistfight just down the street from our house. After getting the worst of the fight, Tommy ran home crying. Several of us kids were playing in the front yard when Joan came home bragging about winning the fight and how badly she defeated Tommy. Before she even finished telling her story, we saw Tommy's mother come charging down the street. We could tell she was mad and was ready to stick up for her son.

Joan ran into the house, hastily telling Mom what happened and we all ran in after her. Mom looked out the window and saw Tommy's mom was getting close.

Mom started heading toward her bedroom as she said, "When Tommy's mother asks for me, you kids tell her I'm not home. Remember, I'm not home."

Tommy's mom stomped up on the porch and banged on the door. Pat answered the door.

"Tell your mother to come talk to me. I want to tell her what a naughty girl Joan has been," she said.

Pat said calmly, "Mom's not home."

All the rest of us kids shook our heads, agreeing with Pat. We wouldn't give Mom away. She wasn't home.

"Well, I'll be back," she said. "I want your mom to know what kind of a bully Joan is. She needs to be punished for picking on Tommy."

We promised to tell both Mom and Dad about Joan's fight. It was useless to tell Joan not to fight and beat up her friends. We knew we were wasting our breath, but we promised we would try.

I don't remember exactly how old Joan was when she quit being a slugger and turned into a lady, but this wasn't the last of her fights.

48. Pat Goes to the Races

A few days before school was out we got a surprise. Dad came home and said to Mom, "A man named Henry Boyer is coming over to talk to us tonight, Gardy." Even though Mom tried to get more out of him, that's all Dad would say.

It was horse racing season on the East coast. The Bowie racetrack was busy, filled with trainers and their horses. The racing season started and ended in Bowie; therefore, it was common to stable many horses there when they weren't racing on another track. The owners of the horses were looking for help. They needed stall cleaners, and people to walk the "hot" horses and feed them. Ben Brady, our landlord, noticed how small Pat was and mentioned it around the track. That's why Mr. Boyer was coming after supper to talk to Mom and Dad about Pat getting a job as an exercise boy.

Mom said, "Pat hasn't even ridden a horse out of a pasture – never sat in a saddle." She was positive Pat would never be an exercise boy and laughed about it until Mr. Boyer showed up. Once she heard Dad and Mr. Boyer talk for a while, Mom realized that Pat just might become an exercise boy. We kids were politely asked to go outside and play...somewhere further than just outside the door so we couldn't eavesdrop.

They agreed Pat could help Mr. Boyer on a trial basis. He would learn how to ride a horse on one of those pancake saddles. That was funny! Who would want to ride a horse on one of those things? If he was good enough, they would have him actually ride on the track to "breeze" the horses. To breeze is to walk, trot or gallop a horse a short distance to cool them off.

Pat would get paid more as he improved. In the meantime, he would clean stalls, feed horses, learn how to put the saddle and halter on a horse, and anything else the trainer asked him to do. Pat might have been small but he was athletic and strong. At the end of the meeting it was decided that Pat would go to the track to help every day. In three days Mr. Boyer would come back to discuss any future Pat may have at the track.

Three days later, when Mr. Boyer returned, he said, "I'm really happy with your boy, Al. How about you let him come live at the track so he can travel the racing circuit? In fact, I think Pat should quit school. He has the makings of becoming a great jockey."

"Quit school?" Mom said. I could tell she was shocked. "No way is Pat quitting school and living at the race track. Al, he is barely fifteen years old! It's unheard of. Pat living at the race track is beyond belief."

But Dad was all for it; and, of course, Dad won the argument. Just like that, Pat went off to live at the racetrack and I had to figure out how to live without my big brother. Before long, Pat was completely hooked for life. He was going to stay at the racetrack forever.

Pat, age 7, atop a plow horse while visiting Grandma and Grandpa Quinn on their farm in Shakopee, MN.
Summer 1938

49. Moving... *Again*

Not long before school was out that year, Dad came home from work at suppertime and we discovered we would have another new adventure. Dad would be changing jobs. He got out of the car and said, "Well, kids, we're moving to Pennsylvania again – to a town called Tunnelton. This time we'll stay a long time."

He walked into the house to tell Mom. We followed him through the door and waited to see what Mom would say about another move. "Gardy, we've got great news. We have a job drilling out a railroad tunnel in Pennsylvania. It will last two years! Can you believe it? Up to two years of living in the same place!"

Mom got that familiar look on her face; the one where I knew she wanted to say, *No, no, I don't want to move one more time!* She stood there waiting for Dad to tell her more details. "It's for the railroad. They pay really good. Just think, we'll be able to finish paying for the farm. Hopefully, we'll have money left to buy some dairy cows. We will finally be farmers!"

Mom stood there thinking it over, then finally said, "Two whole years?"

Dad was beaming. "Yes, two years! This will be our last move before going back to Wisconsin to live on our farm. Then we'll live there until we're old and gray. All these moves have been worthwhile. We have made real progress paying for our farm. Now we can look forward to setting a time to move back. Okay?"

Mom had a sort of half smile on her face. She seemed to be thinking about that one last move. I had heard her say how tired she was of moving...so tired of taking us to another school; only to have to tell them she wasn't sure if we would finish the year. After a long pause, she asked, "We'll only have to move one more time, and that would be back to Rice Lake?"

"That's right. They promised this job would last two years. It's a tunnel through a mountain...a long tunnel. We'll be drilling from both ends to meet in the middle. It will be almost 4,000 feet long. Then, after we meet in the middle, we'll re-drill to make it high enough for a train to travel through it. It's a real big job, with good money."

Dad kept talking, flashing that big Irish smile, and Mom kept listening. I'm not sure she was buying the "no more moving" part, but I could tell she wanted to believe it. I thought, *At least she's not crying this time.* I hated seeing Mom cry. We kids gradually wandered outside to play until Mom called us for supper. We were all full of questions...questions that had only vague answers. We would all have to go to another new school. I guess I would have been going to a new school anyway, since I was at last going to be in high school in the fall. Pat was going to stay at the racetrack when we moved.

During the school year, John became friends with Anthony, one of the men who worked at the school as a handyman. Anthony fixed anything that needed fixing at the school and John loved learning from him. John was a natural at taking things apart and fixing them. He became Anthony's volunteer helper and they became real friends. In fact, on some weekends Dad let John stay with Anthony at his home in Washington, D.C. Anthony owned a couple of apartment buildings and kept John busy taking care of the properties. Anthony told Dad he could sure use John's help for the summer and wanted to know if he could stay with him all summer.

John and Anthony both campaigned to get Dad and Mom to agree. Mom insisted that John was too young, "He's only in the fourth grade," she said. "No kid should be away from home at that age. Pat is gone, probably forever. I can't lose another one of my boys, Al. What are you thinking?"

Dad answered, "It's an opportunity for John to see all of the historical sites in Washington, D.C. He might never get that chance again."

John was a fast talker, and Anthony was also persuasive. In the end, Dad decided that John would stay with Anthony for the summer. John was happy as a lark, but Mom was upset about it. She did reluctantly agree that he could try it until school started. Dad always wanted to give us kids every opportunity to learn something new, but that whole summer whenever we talked about John I could see the pain in Mom's face.

A few weeks later, I woke up and looked around. I thought to myself, *This is our last day in Maryland*. I really liked it here. Going into Washington, D.C. was always fun, except of course the pain when I had to go to the Doctor. I sure hoped I'd never get sick again.

Spending half the winter being sick made it hard to get schoolwork done. That was past and I really felt good now that I had recovered from getting my tonsils out. We were looking forward to me staying well this coming winter. Oh, how I hoped.

I got up, got myself dressed, and headed to get some breakfast. Mom had packed sandwiches and food for us to eat along the way. Dad said we wouldn't be stopping to eat; only for gas and bathroom breaks. I didn't know how far Tunnelton was, but guessed it wasn't any further than it had been getting here from Reed.

As the time approached to get on the road, I thought about leaving everything I loved about living here behind. Being in Washington, D.C. sparked a love for U.S. history that I still have today. Even though I hated to leave, I was looking forward to living in one town for two whole years. It seemed like an impossible dream after having moved so many times.

As we were getting ready to go, Dad said, "Tunnelton is an old coal mining town just outside of Saltsburg. It's only about thirty miles or so from where we used to live in Clymer. The mine is closed, but the houses they built for the miners are real nice. Our new house even has four whole bedrooms upstairs. Can you believe it?"

I couldn't believe it - *four bedrooms!* All of our furniture and belongings would fit in our new house easily. The other places we lived were never big enough for us, let alone our stuff.

John (9), Dad, Joan (11), Pat (15), Romaine (6) and
Uncle Albert, visiting Chesapeake Bay.
Spring 1946

Dad with all of us kids outside our home in Bowie, Summer 1946
Front row: Romaine (6), Dennis (1), John (9) and Ann (4)
Back row: Pat (15), Rose Mary (13), Dad and Joan (11)
Photo Courtesy: Judy Quinn McConnell

TUNNELTON, PENNSYLVANIA
June 1946

50. Tunnelton

When we drove up to our new home, I was disappointed to see it had not been painted since they built it. I had no idea how long ago that was. The raw wood was weathered and dark. Years of dirt and dust from the street and soot from the coal mine stuck to the wood. I thought to myself, *I sure hope it's nicer inside or Mom's going to be disappointed.* From the outside, it looked bigger than most of the houses we had lived in since moving from Markville.

We piled out of the car and started to explore. We all cheered when we saw how big it was inside the house. There was actually a front door for company to enter. Other times our company had to come in past all the stuff piled up in a corner of the kitchen. The living room took up the whole front of the house. We admired the kitchen, pantry and wash room, which was for the washing machine and all our coats and shoes. I looked around but couldn't find a bathroom. Then I saw the little house out back.

Mom was truly pleased with the house and was grinning from ear to ear as she said, "This is one of the nicest houses we've lived in since Markville, Al!" Then she gave Dad a big hug.

We had such a nice house back in Markville, with lots of room for company, a place for us to play and our bedrooms had room for all our toys. It had been a long three years since we moved away from that wonderful house until now.

Our new house was on the end of the street, which made it even better. We didn't have to worry about neighbors complaining when we played and made too much noise. The neighborhood kids always came to our house because Mom never cared how much noise we made. She was happy to know where we were, not wondering which tree we were in or if we were jumping off a wall somewhere.

It didn't take us long to get to know everyone around. It was a long block to the blacktop road, which ran through the town and across the railroad tracks to the depot. A grocery, tavern and restaurant combined with a small post office were next to each other just down the road. The train station accommodated passengers for the trip to Saltsburg and beyond. In 1946, trains were still the main mode of transportation. Owning a car was out of the question for most families. We gladly rode the train again. It reminded us of the wonderful train crews that were our friends back in Minnesota.

Tunnelton had a boomtown atmosphere. The government was building a dam to control the flooding in the Conemaugh River Valley. The dam was being built at the same time the railroad was drilling a tunnel to change the elevation of the tracks. Once the dam was completed, the old tracks would be under water.

Not long after we moved to Tunnelton, Mom came back from getting the mail and said, "We got a letter from Aunt Rose and Uncle Ralph. Come, I'll read it to all of you."

Mom read the letter and we all laughed at some things Uncle Ralph did. He loved pulling jokes on anyone who would fall for them. It was so great to hear news from back home. I dreamed of the day we would move back to Rice Lake to be close to Aunt Rose and Uncle Ralph again.

Later, Mom said to me, "Rose Mary, John at the restaurant asked if you might be interested in helping out while they are busy with extra customers. The crew building the new bridge will be around for a month or so."

"I'd like that. What do they want me to do?" I asked.

"You would clear the dirty dishes off the tables and help serve food when it gets real busy. If you wait on tables, you'll get tips."

"Tips? That would be great! Tell him I said yes."

"You can go over about ten tomorrow morning and talk about it," she said warmly.

"Joan, did you hear that?" I bragged. "I might get to make money. Even better money than babysitting."

"You get to do the good stuff. I wish I could make some money," she pouted.

The next morning, I walked the two blocks over to the restaurant and got hired to be a flunky, as John, my new boss, called it. "You will be clearing the tables. When it's busy you can serve food – it's easier than you think. Most of the steady customers order from the cook."

I soon found out that when regular customers came in they walked past the cook and would say, "Hi

Molly, I'll have the blue plate special."

Molly would yell back, "You bet! Coming right up."

That's when I'd take them a glass of water, and take their drink order. When an order was ready, Molly would say, "Order up," and then tell me where to serve it. I never understood why they called the special of the day the *blue plate special.* We didn't have any blue plates. There were only six tables in the restaurant, so when there was an empty chair, someone sat there.

It was almost like going home for lunch and Mom would say, "Do you want leftover stew or a peanut butter and jelly sandwich?"

Sometimes at the restaurant, you might get a third choice. It was good food and the men didn't have much time so they were always happy. Sometimes when they left to go back to work they'd ask Molly what she was cooking the next day. The menu usually included the choice of a hamburger, tuna salad sandwich, or roast beef dinner. We always had a special; fish with fries, pork chop and mashed potatoes or stew. Once in a while Molly would cook up her special chicken with dressing and sweet potatoes. When the men came back the next day, they knew the food would be ready so they could eat and run.

That summer I worked the lunch shift during the week, a few supper shifts and all day on Saturdays. John was very particular about how I served the food. He taught me exactly how to greet customers and make sure I asked them back. I learned to love being a waitress working for John in that little restaurant. He made work fun because he was having fun talking and joking with the customers.

A DRILLER BITES INTO THE ROCK FACE OF THE PENNSYLVANIA RAILROAD'S NEW SALTSBURG TUNNEL . . . . IT WILL BE 2½

Pittsburgh Sun-Telegraph, July 31, 1946

"A Driller Bites into the rock face of the Pennsylvania Railroad's new Saltsburg Tunnel"

Dad's crew getting started on the railroad tunnel in Tunnelton, PA.

51. Saltsburg High School

All of a sudden it was time for school to start. Now I would be riding the bus into Saltsburg to become a high school student. I stood at the bus stop watching for other kids to come. I thought, *I really miss Pat – oh how I wish he was here to ride the bus with me.* Finally, three girls came up and said hi.

"I'm Sarah. This is Jan and she's Linda," one of the girls said.

"Hi back," I said. "I'm Rose Mary – nice to meet you. I've lived here most of the summer but didn't get to meet but one girl and she isn't here."

Sarah said, "My mom saw you working at the restaurant when she went to pick up our mail. I wanted to come to meet you but I had to babysit."

"That would have been nice. It's great meeting before we get on the bus," I replied. Dad used to take us the first day of school, but now I was on my own. It was nice to have a couple of new friends.

When we got to school, it didn't seem too big to me.

There were around five hundred students in all. As we got off the bus, upper classmen directed the freshmen to our homerooms. The rest of the day we got acquainted with our new teachers and classrooms.

The next day the first thing we did was take an IQ test. After all the school changes I had been through, I was ready for that test. I told one of the students next to me, "Hey, look out, I've taken this same test three times already." I didn't even have to read some of the questions and I remembered a lot of the answers. I easily finished first.

Two days later my homeroom teacher said, "Rose Mary, Mr. Simpson would like you to go to the office. Please go now."

I walked down the hall wondering if something had happened at home. The girl at the front desk motioned me to go right in. As I walked through the door, Mr. Simpson seemed surprised. He looked down at the paper on his desk, looked up at me and said, "I'm sorry, I was expecting a boy."

"Do boys have Rose Mary for a name here?" I asked.

"No, I only looked at your last name. I called you in here to tell you I signed you up for Latin class," he said.

Surprised, I asked, "Why? I had not planned to take Latin."

"Anyone who is college material needs to take Latin. Your IQ test shows you are definitely college material," he said with a smile.

"Thank you. I don't know what to say," I said. I knew I shouldn't tell him about the other times I had already taken the test.

"It's my job to make sure all students who have a high IQ take all classes needed to be ready for college.

Go to room 210 and tell Miss Stanton I sent you. Good luck."

The only thing I knew about Latin was what I had learned at St. Margaret Mary's in Parkersburg. We sang every Mass in Latin.

"This isn't church Latin, students," Miss Stanton said the first day. What little Latin I did know made it somewhat easier for me.

After a few weeks, I discovered that there was a girls' basketball team. I really liked basketball. In Laurel, we played basketball in gym class. We played half-court with six girls according to the rules back then. Girls weren't supposed to have the endurance to play full court. However, here in Saltsburg, we played full court with five players. Best of all, we played teams from other schools.

At first, practice was right after school, which was fine for me because I could ride the train home. After about a week, our practice schedule changed to after supper. What was I going to do after school until it was time for practice? I knew Dad would never let me wander around in Saltsburg for several hours after school four days a week. I was discouraged and tried to think of a solution.

I tried not telling Dad because I knew he would make me quit the team. I missed a couple of days of practice and told some of my teammates why.

Then out of the blue, Helen Troup, our senior team captain, said, "You're coming to my house for supper tonight. You can stay until time for practice. My mom wants to meet you."

I couldn't believe it!

I met Helen after school and we walked together. When we got to her house, she opened the door and called out, "Mom, we're here!"

A smiling lady came into the kitchen and shook my hand. Mrs. Troup stood back, looked me over and said, "Welcome. I've heard that you could turn into a pretty good basketball player."

I stammered, "Thanks for inviting me. My mom and dad were afraid I'd have to quit. They didn't want me hanging around town until it was time for practice."

"You just plan on having supper with us every night there's practice," she said. "We'll be happy to have your company. We'd like to hear all about where you moved from and, of course, if you like it here."

"Really? I can come every night?" I asked. "Thank you so much! I'm so happy I can stay on the team!"

It was a dream come true to be part of a school team. It felt so good and I loved playing basketball. I thought, *How could I be so fortunate to have the best player on the team take me in? I have a place to stay and I have a place to have supper, too.*

The rest of the season, I enjoyed basketball practice, playing in games, the train ride home and most of all, being taken in by Helen's family.

Just like that, our basketball season was over. It was rainy and we didn't have much of a winter.

We did have fun during the winter, though. Sometimes we would go ice-skating on a swamp that froze over. The cattails and other weeds in the swamp made it challenging to skate but it was still a lot of fun. We would light a bonfire, roast marshmallows and play tag until it was time to go home. Some of the kids didn't have skates, so they slid around on their overshoes. No one cared – we just had fun.

Saltsburg High School Warriors - Girls' Basketball Team
Source: La Saltianna Yearbook 1947

Team Captain, Helen Troup
Source: La Saltianna Yearbook 1947

52. Cave-in

Uncle John and Uncle Francis were finally home from the war in the Pacific. Both were happy to be back in the states. Uncle Francis seemed fine, but Uncle John had contracted jungle rot on the Island where he was stationed during the war. Jungle rot is a skin disease more common in tropical heat. It reminded me of leprosy.

Uncle Francis stayed in Minnesota and went back to the job he had before the war. He was happy there because Grandpa and Grandma lived in St. Paul and he was able to care for them. He was single so he took on the job gladly.

Before the war, Uncle John had worked for the Meyers Company along with Uncle Albert. The company was happy to ask Uncle John to come back east to work with them again. Uncle John came to stay with us until there was an opening for him at another jobsite. He was so much fun – always joking and helping. It was my job to split the wood for the cook stove and he took it over for me.

We could use coal, but Mom hated the smell of coal burning in the kitchen. Every time we had to add coal to the stove, smoke billowed out and we'd have to open the door to clear the air. We used coal at night, especially in the potbelly stove in the living room. Coal burned slower than wood so it lasted all night.

After a while, Uncle John and Uncle Albert were assigned to a job in Newark, Ohio. They were happy to be working together. Uncle John thought they might send him back in a few months because the job in Tunnelton would last another year.

We were sorry to see Uncle John go. He would stop and shop for anything Mom needed. He always seemed to bring ice cream. I guess it was because he worked at a creamery for years in White Bear Lake, Minnesota, where they made wonderful ice cream. He must have loved ice cream as much as I did. We always had an excuse to finish it off because we didn't have a freezer. No one in their right mind would let even one spoonful of ice cream go to waste.

I was enjoying life in Tunnelton. I had good friends in school, and Mom was happy that we were going to be living in the same house for two whole years.

We had lots of rain that winter so nothing was frozen. The tunnel Dad was working on was more than three quarters of a mile long. They pre-drilled it ten feet high from both sides of the mountain as a test run to be sure they met in the middle. If they drilled from one side of the mountain, they might end up in the river if they were off by only a couple of degrees. The only technology they had to guide them in those days was a compass. After they met in the middle, they would drill the tunnel to full size.

In late February, I heard a commotion in the hall at school. People were hurrying about and crying. After school, we heard there had been a terrible accident at the tunnel. Then when Dad came home later that day, he was especially dirty. Not only was he dirty, he was terribly sad. He came into the house, sat down at the kitchen table and didn't say a word. We all stopped what we were doing and waited to hear what was wrong.

Dad's hands were shaking, and I could see he was trying not to cry. There were tears on his cheeks when he said, "There was a terrible accident at work today." For a long minute he couldn't speak. When he was finally able to get some words out, he spoke in just a whisper. "There was a cave-in at the tunnel. Two good men died today." It was February 27, 1947.

Dad continued speaking with a deep sadness in his voice. "I was right there. We had to dig to uncover the dozer Jim Shirley was operating. That's how I got this dirty. I could see he was dead right away...he had so many broken bones. When the walls caved in Jim was on the ground checking the rear tire on his machine. I heard him yell. Then silence. Nothing but silence, and so much dust. The dust hadn't settled when people from outside the tunnel started yelling. Yelling for us to say we were all right. I've never been in such a nightmare." Then Dad was silent...sitting there not making a sound, but his whole body was shaking. He couldn't stop shaking. I'll never forget seeing how sad Dad looked sitting there. It broke my heart.

Mom went over and hugged Dad, not knowing what to say. She was crying too. As I watched them try to comfort each other, I was confused. They knew how it felt to lose someone. I had never experienced such sadness before. Mom motioned for us to go into the living room and please be quiet.

I was the oldest child at home now. What would Pat say if he were here? Joan and I mostly just sat there being quiet. The little kids were talking and pushing on each other, gradually getting louder. I had to do something.

I said, "Go upstairs and make sure your rooms are clean. Make sure your homework is finished." I didn't know what else to say.

Joan went to the kitchen door and stood there staring straight ahead. Time passed slowly while we waited for Mom and Dad to tell us what to do.

The sounds coming from the kitchen were as sad as I had ever heard. I don't know how long it took, but Mom started clearing the table. She saw Joan and me standing in the doorway and motioned for us to go upstairs. We went without question. It was a very long night not knowing much of what had happened.

Morning came and Dad was gone before we got downstairs. We got ready and left for school mostly in silence. Everyone at the bus stop seemed to know more than I did. All the kids knew Dad was working at the tunnel. They questioned us as if we should know. I felt sorry that I didn't know.

Our school day was filled with more questions than answers. I discovered that Jim Shirley, the man Dad said had been killed, was Roberta's dad. She was the oldest of seven kids and her twin brothers were my classmates. My mind couldn't comprehend what a tragedy it was for their family. I thought to myself, *Thank you God, I still have my Dad.* I was just fourteen and no thought of *it could have been my Dad* entered my mind. Not even for a second did I let myself think that terrible thought.

By the end of the school day, we heard most of the

details. Dad couldn't bring himself to talk about it and I was smart enough not to ask. The principal told us we would all be able to go to Mr. Shirley's funeral. It was difficult to see our classmates so devastated. As the oldest, Roberta would now be the one her mom leaned on for courage.

During the funeral, I sat in an aisle seat at church. Roberta's whole family sat in front. After the service, they slowly walked out of church following the casket.

Mrs. Shirley was so overcome with grief she was crying out loud. Roberta walked hand in hand with her mom, crying uncontrollably. When Roberta saw me standing by the center aisle, she stopped and grabbed my hand.

She sobbed, "Please, please make your dad quit that job! I don't want your Dad killed, too."

I held her hand gently and said, "I'm so sorry. I wish I could make it easier for you."

She continued, "I'm begging you; please make your Dad quit. Make him go get another job. He can do anything, just not work there anymore."

She hurried on down the aisle to catch up to her family. I was shocked at the thought of losing my dad, too. We all followed the family into the cemetery for the burial service. Afterward, we went back to school and waited for classes to end. The bus ride home was silent and sad.

I never told Dad what Roberta said to me in church...never begged him to quit that job...never said a word. Every night for a week, I heard Mom crying and begging Dad to quit.

"Gardy, nothing is going to happen to me. Remember, when this job is finished, we can move back to Wisconsin. Back to the farm, our farm, across the road from Rose and Ralph. It will be paid off and we'll be able to buy cows. Don't you think I'm looking forward to living there? We're fixing the tunnel so it won't cave in again. Let's talk about our future. Can we please not think about another tragedy? Not another word. We don't want the kids to worry about something that's never going to happen."

Mom cried, "Don't you understand? We are all afraid for you. What will happen to all of us? At least if you're alive we can look forward to a future. I want you to quit."

Dad thought about it for a minute and said, "I can't quit. We need this job. We're not going to talk about it again. I know you're worried. I promise I'll be careful. Please, please let's not talk about it anymore."

They didn't talk about it anymore and we tried not to think about it. We lived a somewhat normal life for a couple of weeks.

About two weeks after the cave-in, I was in history class when our principal, Mr. Simpson, opened the classroom door and said, "Rose Mary, please come out in the hall."

I got up and walked out the door, wondering what was going on. Mr. Simpson was one of my basketball coaches. As soon as I saw him, I knew something was very wrong.

He said to me, "There's been another accident at the tunnel. I'm so sorry to tell you that your dad was killed."

I cried, "No! This can't be true."

Mr. Simpson put his arm around me and led me to the office. From that point on, everything was a blur. I felt like I was living a nightmare.

Why didn't I warn Dad of what Roberta had said? I stayed in the office until it was time to take the bus home since Mom didn't drive.

When I got home all the other kids were already there with Mom. We all hugged and cried for a long time. Mom was in shock and I didn't know how to help her. We were all in shock.

RICE LAKE, WISCONSIN
March 1947

53. Good-bye, Dad

It was March 11, 1947 when Dad and another worker, Ed Quarford, died in a second cave-in at the tunnel. I just couldn't believe it.

The company notified Uncle John and Uncle Albert in Ohio. They immediately packed up their families and drove to Tunnelton. They arrived before nightfall and took charge of making the arrangements to get us all back to Rice Lake, Wisconsin for Dad's funeral.

Pat was at the track in South Carolina when he got the call. He immediately arranged to fly into Pittsburg and then took the train to Tunnelton. When I saw Pat, he seemed all grown up. In less than two days, we were on our way to Wisconsin.

Pat, Mom, Romaine and Dennis accompanied Dad's body on the train back to Rice Lake. Pat, at age fifteen, took charge. He had been on his own only a few months but it was long enough to help him guide Mom through the agony of that train ride.

As we stood there saying good-bye at the train station, I thought, *Here it is, our last day in Tunnelton. In a few minutes, we'll get in the car and go back to Rice Lake. Dad won't be there waiting for us. This is the worst day of our lives. Dad will never be with us again. He and Mom worked so hard saving the money to buy a farm for us so we could live near our relatives. Now we'll be on that farm without him.*

Mom never said anything, but I know how worried she was; afraid that she would not be able to finish paying the mortgage and then where would we go? Pat wouldn't be there to help keep her courage up. I was too young to understand we had no income. I did know that we would get Social Security from the government. I had a friend at school here in Tunnelton whose Dad had died and her Mom got a check every month to help support her. Mom now had six kids to support and all these expenses to get moved back to Wisconsin. The company paid to ship Dad on the train. I couldn't imagine Dad alone in his casket on the trip, when he had almost always been with us on the road.

On the train, Romaine sat staring out the window because Mom cried so hard whenever she tried to speak. Pat made sure they got to the second depot in Chicago and on the same train with Dad. The train ride to Rice Lake wasn't very long, but it was difficult for Romaine and Pat to watch Mom cry. Sometimes Pat had to walk away so Mom couldn't see the tears trickling down his cheeks. At two, Dennis was too young to understand what was happening. At seven, Romaine knew his life was changing forever, but his innocence kept him from understanding the depth of what was happening.

When the train arrived at the depot in Rice Lake,

the hearse was waiting further down the platform.

Pat carried Dennis as they all walked down the platform to be by the hearse. Uncle Ralph was waiting there to give them a ride out to the farm where Dad would be displayed in the piano room. As they stood waiting, curious people gathered to see what was happening. Romaine could hear them talking and asking questions. Just as he was going to tell them they were taking Dad off the train, a man said, "I think there is a casket on the train. Yes, they are taking it off now. I wonder who it is."

"That's my Dad," Romaine said bravely. "We brought him here from Pennsylvania."

The crowd became silent when they heard Romaine say it was Dad. What could they say?

The only sound Romaine could hear was Mom. She was almost screaming, "No, no! Oh, it can't be! It can't be!"

Pat and Uncle Ralph took Mom by the hand and led her to the car. The trip to the farm was slow and silent.

While they were on the train, John, Joan, Ann and I were in a caravan of three cars driving back to Wisconsin for the funeral. It was wonderful to have our cousins, Maxine and Judy, with us. All three cars traveled together in case of any breakdown.

During the car ride, I just stared off into space, trying not to think of the future. *A new school without Pat there to give me courage. A new house out in the country without Dad. Out in the country with a car that Mom can't drive.*

As sad and lost as I felt, I knew Mom was even more desperate. Of course, I didn't really understand until I had my own children to worry about; but I could see the sadness in her face, sadness beyond anything I had ever seen.

I thought about the train ride almost five years ago when we first left Markville. I had sprained my ankle just before the trip and had to hop on one foot. Pat ran ahead to hold the train in Chicago while Mom gathered all us kids to run so we wouldn't miss it. It would have been a disaster for Mom to be stranded in Chicago with six kids. I don't know how she had the courage then for that trip. Now she had seven kids – how would she be able to handle it on her own?

The road back to Wisconsin was the longest trip I have ever taken. I thought about all the stories Dad told us. Stories about when he was catching baseball. The way he threw old Shorty out when he tried to steal second. How he loved it when we were sitting right behind him at home plate so he knew exactly where we were during the game. When he took me to the doctor in D.C. and always made time to go sightseeing. When I woke up in the hospital after having my tonsils out, he was there holding my hand. Dad made time for everything we got involved in, from school activities to getting in trouble.

Our lives were about to change forever. I didn't realize how completely. Rice Lake would be a new chapter, a new way of life. Changes we had no way to prepare for. How would I get through it? How would we all manage without Dad? What if I would have said something to Dad about what Roberta said? What if I had begged him to quit his job at the tunnel? I have never forgiven myself for not trying to get Dad to quit that job before it killed him.

It seemed like months until we got back to Wisconsin. It was cold and snowy when we arrived in Rice Lake. I was too numb to know how to feel. Joan mostly cried. She didn't say much, she didn't talk much; just looked lost and must have felt abandoned by both Mom and Dad. I know I did.

We were tired and hungry when we got to Aunt Rose's house. She had plenty of food waiting. Mom and Pat had gone to see Father at the church in Dobie to make funeral arrangements for Dad. Uncle Ralph took them after he finished milking the cows. When we finished eating, Aunt Rose showed us where we would be sleeping. It was a big farm house and had a spacious upstairs with extra beds for company.

When I woke up the next morning, I could hear people talking downstairs. Then I remembered. *Dad is gone. He's never coming back. They must be telling everyone about the funeral arrangements.* I tried to dress very slowly. I didn't want to think about Dad's funeral. By the time I got downstairs, most of the people were gone. Mom and Aunt Rose were alone in the kitchen. I stopped in the doorway to listen. Aunt Rose had her back to me, washing dishes at the sink. Mom sat on a chair holding Dennis in her lap.

"Hildegard, we'll all help you," Aunt Rose said sweetly. "You can count on us all. You have to be brave."

Mom was crying as she answered, "How will I ever make it? How will I be able to take care of my kids? I just can't think."

Aunt Rose walked over to where Mom was sitting and hugged her. She stood there a moment, tears running down her cheeks. She wiped her eyes and said, "All of us have agreed to pitch in and make sure you won't be left alone. We will keep you all together."

"What will I do?" Mom cried. "If only I could have found a way to make Al quit that job. He promised Tunnelton would be our last move. He promised. I'd give everything if he were here to be with us. He kept his promise all right, he just won't be here to keep us together."

Mom said over and over, "I don't know how to do anything. I haven't worked for anyone, ever; just on the farm and helping out in the grocery store. No one will hire me."

"The money will run out, and then what? We'll lose the farm. We'll be out in the cold. I can't do anything." She was crying so hard her body shook and I could hear the desperation in her voice. I wondered if we would all be farmed out to live with relatives who could afford one or two of us. Tears were on my cheeks when Uncle John came over and gave me a hug.

"Don't you worry," he said. "We'll all see to it you will be cared for and stay together. We have been talking it over; we're making plans. Albert is looking for a business to buy close to Rice Lake so he can keep an eye on you all. You know twins are like that. Your Dad was there for Albert when he had that broken neck. He was ready to take care of Sylvia and the girls. It will work out. You will all be fine."

That made me feel a little better. Soon more people were talking in the kitchen. Uncle Francis was bringing Grandma Quinn and Uncle Emmett from Minnesota the next day. Uncle Ralph told everyone the wake would be tomorrow night and the funeral the next morning. I wasn't sure what a wake was. I guessed I'd find out when the time came.

Another sleepless night and morning brought more relatives from nearby towns. The adults made plans concerning the wake to be held that night here at Aunt Rose and Uncle Ralph's house. Several ladies called to say they were bringing cookies, cake, sandwiches, and other food. Throughout the day I was introduced to many relatives I had never seen before. They were truly wonderful people.

Finally, it was time to milk the cows. Pat went to help Uncle Ralph while we cleaned up the house and got dressed for the wake. Uncle Francis had arrived with Grandma Quinn and Uncle Emmett. Grandpa Quinn didn't come because he was so crippled up with arthritis. Grandma Quinn went right to the piano room where Dad lay in his casket.

I walked over to where Grandma was sitting, rocking beside the casket not knowing what to say. I could not bring myself to look at Dad laying there in that casket – it would make this nightmare too real. Grandma reached for my hand and held it tight. After a while, she told me how much she had loved Dad. I sat on my knees on the floor beside the rocker as she told me about when "the twins" were little and how difficult it was to have twin boys.

"Your dad was the one who talked too much, was always hungry, never wanted to go to bed and needed to be scolded most of the time," she said.

She continued to talk as tears flowed, "He was the one who took things apart to see how they were made. He loved to laugh." Uncle Albert was now standing by us, and chuckled.

"Your dad was always throwing rocks to see how far he could throw them," she said. "Your Uncle Albert liked to listen to others talk, and he loved to read. Sports didn't interest him much. They never looked like twins. Uncle Albert was two inches taller, had straight hair and never told a joke."

Grandma continued, "Though they had different personalities, they spent most of their time together. After they graduated eighth grade they went to the woods to become lumberjacks. Albert didn't like cutting the trees down, but he did love operating the equipment. The time they spent in the woods gave both twins the experience they needed to get jobs working out east. I wasn't happy when they left Minnesota and after Albert had his neck broken, I tried to convince them to come back to Minnesota."

Soon people were coming in to view Dad as he lay there in the coffin. I wandered out and listened to people tell stories about what a great baseball player Dad was, and all the other things he did that they liked about him. Before long, the house was full of people talking and laughing, while others told more stories.

Someone brought a keg of beer to tap. The crowd got louder, more people came and it became a party. I had never been to a wake before. I didn't understand how they could be laughing, singing and dancing when I was so sad. Then I heard Mom's Uncle Olie say, "It's time for the Belly Bump!"

You may have heard of Irish wakes, where everyone gets drunk on whiskey. This was a German wake (Mom's family was German), where everyone drinks beer. Some men moved the table to the side of the room and everyone moved their chairs against the wall so there would be room to dance. I hadn't noticed the music playing until now. It was a sort of two-step.

"Who's up for a belly dance?" Uncle Olie asked. "Who will challenge me?"

There was a lot of laughter, then someone said, "Pete, Joe or Ted! Get up and show Olie you can beat him!"

Uncle Olie was waiting in the middle of the floor. He swayed to the music while he motioned to each of his brothers to come take the challenge. Finally, Uncle Ted came forward. I was about to see the belly bump dance.

Uncle Olie stood at one end of the room and Uncle

Ted stood at the opposite end. They were both swaying to the music, just looking at each other. Someone yelled, "Olie!" and Uncle Olie held his hand up like he had just won a fight. Then someone else yelled, "Ted!" and Uncle Ted did the same thing. With hands clasped behind their backs, they started the dance. They moved closer, then further back, time and again. They grinned at each other the whole time, waiting to make the bump move. Everyone watched closely so they could pick the winner.

Uncle Ted and Uncle Olie got close enough to do a test belly bump, just barely touching bellies. It was clear they both were used to this dance and either one of them could win. Both men were at least two hundred pounds and it was a sight to see. I just stared at them. If either one went down it would make the house shake. Everyone else was laughing and cheering for their favorite.

Several men switched off doing the dance. Nobody won. Nobody fell down. Grandma Quinn was in the piano room listening to all of the commotion. I wondered what she thought. She didn't like dancing; thought it wasn't dignified. The drinking must have been making her crazy. Then I felt her hand on my shoulder as she said, "It's time for you to be in bed. I'd rather you didn't see all this foolishness. Make sure Joan is asleep. She may be sitting on the stairs waiting for you. You know how she hates it when she can't sleep in her bed."

I went to bed not wanting to think about the next day. Even though I was exhausted, it took me a long time to fall asleep.

Early the next morning, I lay in bed knowing it was time to get up. I did not want to get up. I wanted to lay there forever and pretend the whole thing never happened. I could hear people downstairs talking and moving around. I expected to hear Mom call for me to get up when I heard the sound of a car in the driveway. I got up to look out the window. The bedroom window was above the driveway and I could see it was the hearse coming for Dad. In a minute or two I saw the men carry Dad in his coffin and gently place it in the back of the hearse.

I wanted to yell, *Wait! Wait! You can't take him! I'm not ready to never see my Dad again. Please let him stay here!*

I stood there frozen; unable to move, unable to say a word. It was like a dream watching them close the doors and slowly back out of the driveway. Then the hearse started down the road, taking Dad to church for the last time. I don't know how long I stood there looking out the window, in a daze. I heard Mom call for us all to come downstairs and I knew I couldn't delay this dreadful day any longer. It was time to go to church.

Going to the church, sitting through Mass, watching the pallbearers slowly take Dad down the aisle and out to the cemetery was and still is a blur. I was utterly overcome with grief. Dad was my hero and my idol. I loved and respected him with every ounce of my being...and now he was really and truly gone forever. I couldn't bear it.

The rest of that day I felt like I was in a trance, unaware of what was going on around me. Back at Aunt Rose's house, people continued to come and bring more food. They'd come give me a hug and then be gone out the door. Finally, it was night time and most everyone had gone home.

I sat there thinking, *Will this ever be over? Will I ever get used to not having Dad here to make sure every-*

thing is right in the world? I was thankful when it was time for bed. I was so exhausted I fell asleep as soon as my head hit the pillow.

When I woke up the next morning it was snowing. I had forgotten it was still winter. My life was no longer that of a kid and I knew I had to grow up fast so I could help Mom keep us all together. We had to be a family and stay together. That's the way Dad would want it.

I laid in bed, thinking about the things I would miss the most...Dad telling stories about our eagle rides; pretending he was asleep and chasing us around the house at bedtime...sending me to cut my own willow switch when I needed punishment and pretending he didn't have time to use it until *later*...taking me to the junk stores because he knew I loved going with him...always having time to keep us in line at his baseball games or whatever adventure came along. He allowed us to go places and do things, and when we got in over our heads, he welcomed us back asking, "What did we learn?"

He took time off from work to take me to the doctor, and held my hand at the hospital when I was waking from surgery. He loved history and taught me love of country, honesty, courage and to listen to both sides of any issue. Family came first. Now I would be the oldest sister, could I help teach these things to Ann, Dennis and Romaine?

Whenever I saw Dad's wonderful Irish smile and curly hair it made me feel confident that everything would be okay. He had a way of convincing anyone he was teaching, like ball players or golden glove contenders, that they could be the best.

He chose to stay with us instead of going to play pro ball when he was offered a contract. I heard him say, "It would have been fun to be a St. Louis Brown, but not if I couldn't take my family along." I didn't realize what it meant then; I just knew his favorite thing was being a catcher. A catcher who could throw the ball to second base without getting out of his crouch. He must have had a signal for the pitcher to *hit the dirt* because when he threw to second base the ball was almost a pitch it traveled so fast and low to the ground. When Dad was behind the plate, no one could steal second base.

He made ordinary things fun and laughing a way of life.

In the coming months and years, we all would need every ounce of courage we could summon to get through life without Dad. I was afraid I wouldn't know how to help Mom, but I promised myself I would do everything in my power to keep our family together.

The fateful Saltsburg Tunnel after it was completed.
Circa 1950
Photo Courtesy: Judy Quinn McConnell

Acknowledgement

I thank everyone who helped me remember details for this book and for those who donated pictures. I feel blessed to have known so many wonderful people in my life. I remember you, even your faces, and would be so happy to talk to you again.

Special thanks to my daughter, Jeanine Hansen, for countless hours of editing and asking me questions about why certain things happened, what was said, and how I felt. Because of her, this book is much better than I ever imagined it could be.

Earlier this year, I lost my good friend and writing confidant, David Laster. May he rest in peace knowing how thankful I am for his encouragement and telling me I had a writer's voice.

Please contact me at:

RosemaryQuinnGabriel@gmail.com

Don't miss the first book in *The Quinn in Me* series by RoseMary Quinn Gabriel:

KIDS ON THE LOOSE
An Autobiography

Little House on the Prairie meets *The Waltons* in Rose-Mary Quinn Gabriel's account of her childhood in rural Markville, Minnesota in the 1930's and early 1940's. In this heartwarming true story, RoseMary shares the adventures of small town life in a setting where kids had freedom to climb trees, swim in rivers and roam the countryside. Get to know the Quinn family and share in their escapades as the kids get in and out of trouble. Sure to become an American family classic, *"Kids on the Loose"* will capture your heart and imagination.

Available on Amazon.com and other online retailers.

Made in the USA
Monee, IL
29 September 2021